# Empath Healer

The 13 principles of
healing presence

## LYSA BLACK

*Also by the Author:*

# Heart Healing:
## The 13 principles of emotional self healing

# Divine Purpose:
## The 13 principles of ascension

# Empath Healer:
## The 13 principles of healing presence

## by Lysa Black

### First edition – published 2019

## Disclaimer

whether such errors or omissions result from negligence accident or any other cause.

The author of this book does not dispense medical advice or prescribe the use of any technique detailed in the text as a form of treatment for either physical or medical problems, without the advice of a physician either directly or indirectly. The intent of the author is only to offer information of a general nature, to assist readers in their quest for emotional well-being and personal happiness. In the event that you use any of the information in this book for yourself, the author assumes no responsibility for your actions; neither does the author assume any responsibility in the event that the reader uses any information or techniques to advise or guide others. This book is not intended as a substitute for medical advice from a physician. The reader should regularly consult a physician in matters relating to his/her health and particularly with respect to any symptoms of concern which may require diagnosis or medical attention.

# Dedication

To my dear friend Emma Newborn: your willingness to hear me and stay with me when my soul needed to express itself showed me the true power of healing presence.

When you didn't say anything, (but I knew you heard everything and still needed to reply with nothing), I was changed. I acknowledge, accept and return your love. When we are loved, we change in a way that is unforgettable.

Thank you for investing your presence in me - I saw reflected back the true value of what I knew was precious to give, even though it was something I had never received from a woman before.

We rise and grow as we are seen, loved and truly known!

# *Acknowledgements*

To my precious horse Playly - watching you conceive and bear a foal, only to lose her the next day, tested my resolve to stay in the truth of my deeply feeling heart. The grief was deep and the loss was so significant, yet it was only a foreshadow to your own unexpected death just 2 weeks later. I know you will watch over my family always. You were someone on this earth who saw me in my truth, you received me so fully, and I felt how you could take all of me in. Your example taught me true love and your healing presence was the greatest gift an animal could bestow. I shared only 4 years with you on earth, but you will be a part of my soul family forever. Thank you for showing me my depth, my courage and beckoning me to start jumping fences; you showed me it was time to live and start leaping high over the boundaries that used to keep me in – you were always so fearless!

My dear husband, you always believe in me. You remind me when I'm lost, that I'm just trying too hard. You gently reassure me that I can release all of my 'efforting' and really just allow everything to work out beautifully. Knowing that you find it so easy to love me has set a new standard for what I can allow in my life.

To my son Orion, thank you for reminding me that 'things tend to work out for our family' – you coined that phrase and ushered our family into a new level of ease and trust. Your innate compassion and gentle care has shown me the power of a pure loving child; your love has allowed me to stop trying to 'parent' and simply be who I am within our family.

To my daughter Bow - as soon as I held you, I knew my life was going to start again! You would make me giggle and laugh when you were just a babe. You burst with so much life that I feel I've initiated a second childhood - jumping, running and laughing so hard that we cry. This has allowed me the freedom to finally get so lost in joy that time actually feels as though it stops! You show me how to truly live in and enjoy every moment - I didn't know that this was possible until I met you!

I only knew of 'love at first sight', but Jasmine Fuller - you were 'friend at first sight'! I'm so thankful that we were drawn together, that all of the crazy, unique, dreamy and ambitious parts of ourselves finally found a safe space to settle and make sense. Knowing you are on the planet makes it easier for me every day. I feel so normal around you, it's refreshing!

To Darlene Pearks and Di Crawford-Errington - our spiritual quests, open hearted dining and 'come as you are' and 'receive what you need' generosity has given me such a sense of safety around receiving. It feels as simple as breathing to find myself accessing exactly what I didn't know I required when I am near you both. Finally feeling so heard and understood quenched a hunger I didn't know how else to placate previously.

Anna Linder, your willingness to bravely share your soul genius has given me a visual identity that aligns perfectly with who I am. I now feel completely at home sharing my heart online worldwide. Thank you for this gift of acceptance and comfort.

Stacey Milich Smith, thank you for the beautiful photography you have done for me. Your ability to capture my essence so beautifully has supported me to be seen in a whole new way (and given such a beautiful cover to this book!). Your creativity, sense of adventure and photographic skills have blessed me immensely.

Jean Haner, your dedication to the art of energy clearing and face reading gave me my first clear reflection of my true nature. Finding the ease to prosper from my truth is a gift your presence bestowed upon me. I hope that my presence can likewise become the seeds that can carry forward the blessings of this ancient wisdom that you have devoted yourself to.

Carin Newbould, without your caring heart witnessing these words, I simply couldn't share this book with the world. Thank you for the expertise you've invested in translating my expression into a comprehensible written construct. Knowing my heart can speak to my audience with clarity because of your personal dedication means the world to me.

And finally - to every one of my precious clients who have allowed me to guide them on their path, I am eternally grateful for the trust you have placed in me. This book is a reflection of the victories, bravery and soul strength you all have all shown, to move through great personal adversity to become individuals who can offer healing presence. Professionally standing beside each of you is such a deep soul delight for me - you are all revealing what's truly possible for us all. In your growth and healing, I too can grow and heal. In your development, I develop further as an Empath. I feel tremendous gratitude for those who gave me permission to write their stories and fill this book with real life examples of individuals who used their Empath nature to cultivate healing presence.

# Letter to my fellow Empaths

My name is Lysa Black and I'm an Empath. I can feel the emotions of others within my body. The major challenges of my life have all been centralised around my identity as an Empath. My professional career has been dedicated to my kindred tribe for 10 years, and no matter how my business evolved, it has always been Empaths who have hired me. So I have realised that it's time for me to shine a light on the endemic challenges that Empaths face throughout their lifetimes; in doing so, we can begin to comprehend that the challenges that accumulate in our lives are all pointing to a calling for us to acknowledge our true nature.

This isn't easy. I felt cursed when my abilities came rushing through to the surface after 23 years of active repression. Something unhinged and I couldn't deny my true nature anymore – it was as though an internal dam was released and everything came flooding to the surface as an overwhelming torrent. It was so incredibly frightening and because so few people knew how to help me (and I struggled to know where to look for an explanation), I believed I was beyond help! But I never believed I was beyond heavenly help, so my prayers became incredibly sincere as I was forced into surrender.

I could sense and feel the pain in others, but I couldn't heal until I was willing to claim my own pain which was reflected in those around me. I fell into relationships with wounded men. They were incapable of perceiving my truth, while being lost in a never ending yearning for my care. I woke up and recognised these lost little boys and chose to heal my own heart and not enter a relationship again until I found a man who knew himself sufficiently to be able to truly perceive me.

I was able to reflect on my twenties and understand that I had felt a huge sense of responsibility to nurture my own mother because I loved her so much. At that time, I believed that if I could love her enough, she might change and finally be able to become the mother I longed for, who could nurture me in the way I desired. I attempted to provide for my father, for the same reason; if I could support him enough, maybe he would become someone who would support me? The worthlessness we can feel within us doesn't actually originate from our own bodies or experiences – it's something we pick up through our perception of what lies deep within those near us.

At that time, I believed my worth was earned through service. I felt that kind deeds, acts of service and love to humankind were the only ways I could earn my right to exist, so that was where I lost myself. I gave myself endlessly to others, serving, loving, and helping as much as I possibly could - and in doing so, forgot about myself entirely! Sadly, in losing myself, I found bitterness and resentment – I began to despise people and I knew that meant I was out of balance.

Repeatedly exposed to the 'purge and run' left me awe-struck; the sheer volume of horrific stories of cruelty and deep harm would find me wherever I went. Strangers, friends and colleagues would confide in me so regularly that I became convinced that the world was a cruel and unkind place. Retreating into my "inner cave", I found a new companionship with self-pity. Eventually, after enough time spent feeling sorry both for myself and everyone around me, I realised that maybe nobody else needed more mercy or compassion more than me?

At the time, I was distracting myself by over-indulging in food, men and exercise in an attempt to ignore my own inner world. My binge eating disorder became a reflection of my rejected needs, to the point that it was so rampant I could clearly accept that my rational mind was not in charge of my conscious choices. I would continue to betray and sabotage myself until the pain was sufficiently loud enough for me to stop and pay attention.

Running towards experts, authorities and books did little to quench the yearning within. I finally worked out for myself that I was potentially choosing to suffer by over-consuming food; so that I could ignore the knowledge I had access to within. Maybe there was something within me that was deserving of my attention and reverence? This one idea shifted me out of shame and ushered in an era of mercy. The more love, forgiveness and compassion I applied to myself, the more pain slipped away from my bones like unshackled chains. I was free to feel the truth in others. I knew how they felt and I could give them guidance towards the space to accept themselves, their past and the current state of their lives. I could finally admit that I was an Empath, and use the awareness of what I knew to start to see myself.

Being a witness to pain and suffering only endures for as long as it takes us to see our own pain reflected back. As soon as we forgive ourselves, accept our nature and offer ourselves ceaseless compassion, we begin to comprehend that all of the problems upon which we judged ourselves can disappear; we must simply allow ourselves to be who we really are with no more self-directed control, subjection, denial or manipulation! Once we step into our being and "own our truth", we immediately begin to emanate healing presence; the ability to simply "be" is so deeply grounded in our truth that spontaneous healing manifests within ourselves and everyone around us. (This same healing presence is also a strong deterrent to anyone who cannot receive our presence. Our being will cause them to leave.)

I have now crafted a life specifically designed to support me to thrive in my true nature and I want the same for you. I want us, as Empaths, to recognise, accept and develop our remarkable abilities to bless our own lives and the lives of everyone near us. My pain commanded my attention sufficiently to allow me to lovingly carve out a singular path to follow home to my true nature. Your path will be different, but the destination is the same - self-love, celebration and the opportunity to use our gifts to help others, as well as ourselves. We are Empath healers; let's uncover the 13 principles of healing presence together.

*With love*

*Lysa*

# Table of Contents

# Introduction

## The Starfish Story

*I* was heading into the local supermarket to grab a few random items from the grocery store; it was one of those days where my mind was occupied with the minutiae of daily life. As I walked through the entrance doors, I suddenly became aware of a vision that was unfolding in my mind's eye - a scene appeared that seemed to flash bright for only a few minutes. I had the strongest feeling that what I was seeing held deep significance for me.

I want to share what I saw with you, because I believe it holds deep significance for all Empaths. It only came in a flash, but it has now guided me for over four years, leading me to the conceptualisation and application of the principles in this book. Across this time, I have been experimenting and using what I received from the vision both personally and professionally, and through my experience I have come to fully appreciate the purpose, mission and power of what it is to be an Empath.

My vision opened up on a scene with a little girl walking along the beach, sand dunes spread out on the left hand side and gently lapping blue waves to her right. The transition from lighter dry sand on the left slowly darkened to freshly wet sand on the right by the shoreline.

In this vision, I could only see the back of a little girl; she looked young, only 6 or 7 years old. I was fascinated by the way in which she was performing the same movement, over and over, as she bent down to collect stranded starfish. She would pick one up, then use her little arm to toss it with all of her strength and return the starfish to the waters. This scene brought both a sense of deep appreciation for her kindness as well as a sense of overwhelm and pity, as my vantage point captured the greatness of the task before her. There were thousands of starfish strewn all over the beach. The devotion and dedication of this small child struck me deeply, as I viewed how carefully and joyfully she bent down low every few steps to pick up another starfish.

This was a reflection of a story I remembered from somewhere before; an idea that we need to diligently help those who need assistance, irrespective of the grand scale or difficulty of that endeavour. The question arose within me 'Is she making a difference?', as I acknowledged the vastness of the task, seeing the thousands of strewn starfish that she was hopelessly incapable of rescuing. The story goes on to admonish the power we have as individuals, reminding us that we can make a difference through our personal contribution. For every one of the starfish picked up in that little girl's hands that was thrown back, was truly saved.

I later did research to uncover why masses of starfish can end up stranded on the shores of beaches across the globe. The culprit is simply stormy weather: with no ability to swim, starfish have suction like feet that they use to crawl along the seafloor. In a storm, the violent waves and stronger currents are able to lift up the sea creatures and they end up being dumped on the shore with very minimal capacity for movement. They are at the mercy of the waves to take them back out to sea, if they do not perish or succumb to predators in the meantime.

I instantly knew what this scene was attempting to convey to me: it is a symbolic representation of Empaths. The starfish represent those stranded, lost or disadvantaged, that we feel called to help in the form of assistance, compassion or support. People in need of help can appear to be as vast and numerous as the starfish washed up on the sand in my vision.

In this next unfolding development of my vision, I saw something that I had never seen before. After I had viewed the small girl and this scene of thousands of strewn starfish, the scene evaporated with white wispy gradients, gradually transforming, until my focus zoomed in on one single starfish; in my revised perspective, no little girl was present. Unexpectedly, the starfish in view began to glow, a warm light covered the creature, and it began to 'quake and shake' like a glass of water in a mild earthquake. After this, the starfish began to rise and turn gently in a clockwise spiralling motion, until it was a foot high into the air. I was mesmerized by this scene but giggled, knowing that logically, starfish have no aeronautical capacity! But as continued to watch the scene unfold, I was astonished. Just as the first starfish was only around a foot in the air, 3 out of the 6 nearby starfish suddenly began to glow with golden light and quiver, before they too started a slow and gentle ascent into the air. The scene exploded into a rising cascade of glowing starfish before my eyes. This one starfish had set off a supernatural sequence of hundreds of rising starfish, stretching far across the expanse of the shoreline. As more starfish rose higher, the pattern continued to surge, with more and more starfish rising high into the air.

This vision lasted just a few short minutes, but it somehow conveyed a depth of magnitude to my heart that has instructed and guided me with great significance ever since. As someone who perpetually aided those I found stranded along my way, I know how overwhelming and frightening it can be to consider whether my own contributions were insignificant or pointless? The sheer volume of help needed on a daily basis was more than I had the time, energy and resources to attend to; yet I was incapable of turning away completely from the plight I was witness to in so many around me. The contrast between the little girl's heartfelt individual service that could never meet the need and the golden twirling succession of starfish blew my heart wide open and completely consumed my attention.

Since then, my fascination with this vision has been guiding me to shift from my natural inclination to stop, rescue, help or hear people that I've passed by on my way. I have felt inspired to learn how to simultaneously offer compassion to myself and to everyone around me. Consciously witnessing them, seeing their truth and believing in their ability to rise, I have practiced withholding judgment, refusing to label anyone before me, and instead see them as capable, wise and powerful beings. As I invest my attention on holding myself in the centre of my truth and radiating compassion to myself and everyone close by me, I have noticed effortless shifts, miracles and transformation in those around me while I 'do' nothing other than 'be'. This vision inspired me to develop a series of significant shifts that can redirect our helpful, generous hearts; restraining from rescuing, fixing or lifting the burden of others, instead guiding us to focus our power to owning our true nature, so that we can generate healing presence. After decades of investing laborious, tedious and impossibly hard work trying to make a difference everywhere I go - and struggling with the way in which that made me feel - I now advocate a new way to find a sense of ease, lightness and embodied purpose through culti-vating our natural healing presence.

# Chapter 1

## "The Curse" or "The Calling"?

*When we are willing to trust those around us to find their own way to reconcile their pain, we can hold people accountable for their direct actions – no matter what privately prompts them from within.*

*Our unique perspective provides a lens that reveals far more beneath the surface that most people are willing to admit.*

*E*very Empath initially concludes that they are deeply flawed, impossibly broken and fundamentally weak. This couldn't be further from the truth! These conclusions are the by-product of self-judgment, coming from the pain we feel when our ability is activated and we gain awareness of our gift. This dawning recognition that we are very different to those around us initially triggers self-blame, when we assume that we are somehow fundamentally 'wrong'. We interpret 'feeling emotions so deeply' and being 'heavily impacted by the emotions of others' as flaws and recognise how consistently these elements influence our daily lives. Empaths feel the emotions of others inside of their own bodies. This unacknowledged ability presents five core challenges every Empath will face:

**Emotional confusion** - not knowing which feelings are yours and which belong to another.

**Emotional overwhelm** - feeling so 'full' of feelings that we become inert and have to lie down.

**Emotional pain** - feeling the physical, emotional and spiritual pain of others within our own bodies.

**Social phobias** - feeling afraid of being around people, especially crowds.

**Despondency** - feeling so overwhelmed by the state of the world that we can't show up for the people we love and care for.

Desiree was a gentle and soft spoken Taiwanese woman, who was experiencing confusion around the huge amount of emotional pain that was rising up in her body. Desiree was struggling to process a fluctuating cascade of emotion and wanted mentoring to help her to navigate her internal world and find a sense of stability and peace within. Sometimes she knew what she was feeling, and at other times experienced an overwhelming mixture of feelings that became indiscernible and overwhelming. Needing to take time off work and lie down quietly was a coping strategy Desiree was forced to resort to when she became concerned by a growing sense of powerlessness and no way to understand what was happening. She was, understandably, feeling deeply vulnerable whenever the unknown onslaught of complex emotions surfaced within her.

Professionally, Desiree worked as a Counsellor; it was her rewarding investment in helping others that really gave her a true sense of contribution. Desiree knew her Empath abilities gave her insight and awareness for the troubled family cases that came before her; with her ability to perceive the unspoken trauma, invisible family dynamics and secret concerns in those before her, Desiree could create a soft space for new solutions to present. By simply showing up at a meeting, new perspectives would emerge and hearts would soften, despite the quite alarming and disturbing situations of some troubled teens and their supportive parents.

However, in her personal life there was no sense of purpose, appropriate placement or peace. Desiree's contribution in her own family was neither recognised nor appreciated. Consequently, Desiree felt like she was at times a disturbance, an actual irritation to her family members. The sense that she might be an unwanted and unappreciated burden hurt her deeply. I've found that it's common for Empaths to be more appreciated by a stranger or employer than by their birth family. The ability Empaths have to discern the genuine emotions in others means that whatever is beneath the surface will be revealed; any cloaked agendas become exposed and the truth is made apparent, often exposing private and personal information that some would prefer to keep hidden. Because it is in our nature to sense, feel and perceive the truth in others, our ability can be a real inconvenience for those who wish to keep their inner world private. An Empath doesn't need to have an intention to pry or expose private information - simply being near them means that anything hidden, suppressed or present is easily discernible and recognisable.

As a child, Desiree has been raised by a whole village of family members: two aunts, a grandmother and her mother − all of whom were very strong and capable women who really took care of Desiree. The physical needs of the children in this family were always provided for; it was the lack of emotional availability that had Desiree really feeling unsure about all the feelings inside of herself. On the surface everything that she needed seemed to be supplied, which was one of the reasons why it was so difficult to feel so much inside that just didn't make sense.

Desiree was always very conscious of her mother's inability to be physically demonstrative, but fortunately she was able to appreciate that her mother had her own way of showing love. Desiree's ability to perceive the emotions beneath the surface allowed her to feel how seemingly simple acts could translate a great weight of truth - Desiree learn to trust her mother's love for her, as even when it didn't seem present, it was. When the adults were not around, Desiree would unknowingly step into the mother-figure for her younger siblings. Doing her best to support her family, Desiree would sometimes oversee the behaviour of her younger sister. Desiree knew that her mother had not felt very close or connected with her own mother (Grandmother Lucy) and the past pain and difficulties towards those years was something that Desiree knew prevented her from being able to display and relay her love. Desiree was able to feel within her own body the sense of isolation and hardship that her Mother had endured; she had so much compassion for her and was able to put aside her yearning for what she wished her mother could've provided and instead chose to accept their relationship for what it was. Desiree learnt to rely on her emotional perception to interpret the events in her family; it was only as she got older that she realised that some other members of the family were not able to discern what was happening from the same perspective.

Desiree's younger sister Samantha was seven years her junior and was blissfully unaware of the emotional dynamics of the family. While Desiree became prematurely responsible, her sister was free to enjoy herself and become lost in play. Desiree felt a weight of obligation on her to be more 'obedient' and 'mature'. She had an insight into the feelings and individual perspectives of her family members, and developed a way of bending and adapting around them all to be as accommodating as possible. Knowing how much her whole family had suffered only motivated Desiree to try harder to not be a burden. Samantha was less aware of the intricate dynamics of the wider family; she had no idea her own mother had felt disconnected from her mother too. Samantha couldn't appreciate Desiree's 'good girl' position and she would unknowingly undermine her, make light of her sister's position and be inconsiderate. Some of Samantha's comments were passed just beneath the hearing level of everyone else around them, but Desiree didn't want to complain or bother her parents; she was mindful of their burdens and responsibilities. Her intention was to support and lighten their load, not complain or bemoan her little sister's behaviour. What did it matter how she felt, when everyone else was struggling with things that felt far more significant and worthy than some unkind words?

Some 20 years later, Samantha was still occasionally inconsiderate and unsupportive towards her sister. Desiree on the other hand was keenly aware of Samantha's feelings, knowing exactly how much Samantha had felt abandoned and unloved by their mother, as they had never really been able to perceive each other's love. Desiree could sense how her heart had been required to "toughen up" with very little emotional support. The lack of nurture and care she had been afforded had affected Samantha's ability to be considerate toward her older sister. While, through her understanding, Desiree had found her own unique connection with her mother, Samantha felt unattached and slightly adrift. Desiree had a sense of guilt that she had found a way of connecting with their mother, while no-one had been able to fulfil this role for her beloved sister. These details were not something the pair ever discussed; it was the unspoken emanation that Desiree could feel through her Empath abilities. Desiree was always sympathetic to Samantha, giving her an allowance, accepting her casual and at times slightly disrespectful nature. The thought of being unkind or uncaring towards her sister made Desiree feel sick to the stomach. Being so mindful of the suffering of others, it's common for Empaths to put themselves through great personal strain, in order to prevent anyone else experiencing any more 'additional suffering'.

After another family occasion where Samantha had raised her voice and been dismissive towards her, Desiree felt a stabbing sensation in her heart that jolted her. The disrespectful remarks being generated by Samantha had finally become intolerable. In our Mentoring work, I was able to witness how Desiree was over-compensating for Samantha and tolerating her unintentionally hurtful behaviour because of the pity and love she had for her sister. With the intention of being compassionate and kind, Desiree realised that she had been accommodating Samantha's disrespectful behaviour. I was able to commend Desiree for how beautifully she could invest her Empath gifts in the families she served professionally. She was not personally involved in their situation, which gave her a real impartiality on the scene; this slightly removed perspective allowed her to speak truthfully and relay guidance that would possibly create more pain in the short-term, but actually alleviate the cause, so that the situation could recover in the long run. Guiding her clients to face the truth of the present in order to help them to improve in their future was much easier than this context.

I lovingly challenged Desiree to consider if it genuinely was 'compassionate' to permit her sister to be disrespectful? I affirmed that there is never any acceptable rationale for tolerating disrespectful behaviour. By ignoring disrespectful actions we are silently condoning them. I could feel the hurt that Desiree accepted internally through her attempt to 'minimise' the suffering for her sister and invited Desiree into a new level of honesty within herself. Together we began to open to a new perspective on the situation: in essence, Desiree was amplifying the amount of suffering involved, by forcing herself to endure even more personal pain under the noble intention of shielding her sister. Desiree wasn't actually protecting her sister from suffering; she was accepting additional suffering on her behalf in a vain attempt to show her love. Rather than minimising the pain and suffering in this situation, she was paying a personal price to exacerbate it.

Together we spoke about how love is actually a willingness to trust others to endure their own suffering. I explained that our unique role as Empaths permits us to witness and view the suffering of our loved ones first hand; and while we would give anything for the power to take away the pain of those we love, it's absolutely necessary to set clear boundaries and hold everyone accountable so that they have no power to inadvertently harm us when they are caught up in their own suffering. Acknowledging how unkind and harmful it was for Desiree to accept being disrespected created a liberating shift for her out of self-neglect. Together we discussed how loving it is to speak the truth and hold other people responsible for their behaviour – no matter who they are.

It took a few months for Desiree to generate the courage to respond to her sister differently. Then, at a family dinner, Samantha made a hurtful comment in passing, and Desiree held her peace while preparing a neutral response. At the end of the evening, Desiree walked her sister privately to a taxi, looked her sincerely in the eyes and said *"When you spoke to me in that way, I just shut down, I stop listening. We need to find a middle road, so we can really hear each other."*

Confronted by Desiree's calm approach, Samantha was taken aback, *"Well, it was only a joke! Don't take it so seriously"* she replied defensively, trying to casually skirt out of the conversation. Desiree decided to open up and allow herself to be vulnerable. *"Please don't speak to me as though I don't feel so deeply – because that part of me is never changing."* Over the following weeks and months, Samantha's behaviour changed. Desiree was astounded - finally able to reconcile that while she was sympathetic towards her sister, she was not responsible for her situation or actions. She did not need to accept being treated unkindly in order to try and prevent any more additional suffering for Samantha.

Knowing how to navigate our personal response to the behaviour of others is a struggle for all Empaths. Do we respond to their direct external behaviour, or do we respond to the truth of what is prompting their external behaviour from within? It can be isolating to perceive so much emotional depth and complexity when there are very few people capable of corroborating this information with us. Being over-accommodating with others and sacrificing ourselves to supposedly alleviate their suffering are ways that we limit our presence and diminish our influence. When we are willing to trust those around us to find their own way to reconcile their pain, we can hold people accountable for their direct actions – no matter what privately prompts it from within. Our unique perspective provides a lens that reveals far more beneath the surface that most people are willing to admit. As we are able to acknowledge our purpose to witness the truth, Empaths can open up to a new set of response parameters. We can absolve ourselves of any guilt, and open to honour and protect ourselves in this world, so that we can feel safe, self-accepted and free to nurture ourselves. The repercussions of dishonouring ourselves are so severe that it is imperative that we transition from viewing ourselves as "cursed", to accepting and celebrating ourselves as "called".

# *Healing Guidance:*

1. List the **judgments** that you have labelled yourself because of your Empath nature.

   *(For example - 'Too sensitive', 'Weird', 'Strange', 'Too emotional', 'Irritating' or 'Annoying')*

2. Tell yourself the **truth you want to believe** about who you are and what your function is.

3. What are the three top ways you can **deepen into honouring yourself**, so that you can thrive as an Empath?

   *(Suggestions: Give yourself space/time to be alone, require respect in all of your dealings with others, set clear boundaries and communicate them with others, choose to invest in relationships based on reciprocity, give yourself the freedom to be honest and vulnerable etc.)*

# *Healing Affirmations:*

- *I accept my unique role as an Empath*
- *My gifts give me a unique perspective that is different from most*
- *I am perfectly designed to fulfil my purpose*
- *I'm willing to accept my true nature*
- *I am here to witness and perceive the truth*

# Chapter 2

# Perceiving Pain or Sensing Truth?

*We prefer to feel their feelings over our own, because so few people were able to stay with us in our own true emotions - there is a residual stigma attached to feeling what is within us, because we were often left alone and unaided in those moments.*

*E*mpaths are capable of discerning the emotions within others - not just how they are currently feeling and thinking, but also the emotional pain emanating from the pivotal events in their past. So many people are actually betrayed, hurt or abandoned in moments that others may not even register or recognise as 'difficult'. This repeated exposure to the myriad forms of suffering can validate Empaths and help us to become sensitive and compassionate to the subtle and personal ways that pain comes to us all. All pain offers us a form of truth and wisdom that is not yet known to us; our privileged role as Empaths is to witness and offer non-judgement to the point that we can perceive the truth. We cannot witness the truth fully in others until we can also receive it from our own suffering.

Selene was a witness for so many around her, because her compassionate air of acceptance was a welcome refuge to those feeling scared, upset or in need of reassurance. Her ability to withhold judgement and create a soft space for others to express their true feelings was something Selene was loved for. Being able to perceive what others were feeling through her Empath nature meant that facades could drop and a cascade of genuine emotion could flow forward. It was a deep love for others that birthed this desire to offer gentle acceptance to those caught up in their own suffering - but that was only one half of it! The other half of Selene's desire came from her own past, of being unheard and unseen as a young girl. As someone who lost a sibling at a young age from a terminal illness, her whole family was so awash with grief and loss that there was simply no room and no one capable of witnessing or assisting with Selene's suffering.

Jason was just two and a half years old when the family received a diagnosis of his condition; the next three and a half years were a long preparation for his passing. Selene's mother Cathy became so fixated on her

ding loss that she was not able to truly perceive the fear and
her two daughters or to help them with their own emotions
eir brother's illness. Cathy was understandably determined to
give her youngest and only son a series of joy-filled experiences during
what remained of his life. Family togetherness, adventures into nature
and an abundance of gifts at Christmas were all ways that this family
were able to create memories to reflect the lasting importance of Jason's
life. As the preciousness of each moment encumbered upon their minds
perpetually, the desire for feelings of joy, love and togetherness became
the preferred emotional states when loss, grief and separation were
impending. Our exposure to certain emotional parameters can polar-
ise our experience; the propensity towards seeking joy was heightened
whilst the fear of loss grew ever greater.

Family moments filled with laughter, giggles and deep embraces were
favoured and sought after, while any disclosure or admission of sadness was discouraged. It became shameful to feel sad or cry, which
led Selene to believe that her true feelings were a shameful 'burden'
which should be hidden and kept down, out of public sight. For an
Empath, it's important to recognise that it's our own personal suffering that develops our ability to translate and witness others first.
Initially, it's the preference to feel what others are feeling emotionally that beckons us into the emotional inner world of friends, family members or strangers. We prefer to feel their feelings over our
own, because so few people are able to stay with us in our own true
emotions - there is a residual stigma attached to acknowledging what
is within us, because we were often left alone and unaided in those
moments. This births the desire to never leave another to endure the
same fate.

Selene sought me out as a Mentor to assist her when the overwhelm
and burden of her own experience became greater than she could
bear. Anxiety and depression were extending beyond the confines of
her comfort and Selene sought someone who had likewise endured

childhood difficulties, who could support her to find the healing power of compassionate presence. In one appointment, we both felt led to give our full love and attention to the many times when Selene had cried alone. Being able to stand by her and to witness the depth of loneliness and all of the shame that had been pushed down was immense. Having the presence of another human being allowed Selene to experience her grief and sadness in a way that permitted her to follow the depth of it until it passed.

An Empath like Selene will have a backdrop of emotional complexity residing within her that will find its equal counterpart in another externally. As unlikely as it seems, eventually we will receive into close proximity someone who reflects our particular resonance of emotional pain. For the first time, our motivation to witness and feel the pain within another collides with a re-lived experience of our own suppressed emotion surging to the surface seeking cathartic release. For an Empath, this is when the barrier between ourselves and the world crashes down in alarming splendour. The illusion that we are separate and insignificant is washed away as we witness our own pain appear before us, mirrored in the experience of another.

The truth is that the undefined and unacknowledged terrain of our suffering seeks acknowledgement. It cares not for the focal point of where you choose to invest your compassion, because ultimately all pathways converge to the same blessed outcome. As our companions can bask in our ability to witness their trauma in love without flinching, they are supported through the assistance of our brave presence to unpack their most horrifying moments and recognise that they were not as unbearable and unendurable as they had once presumed. The more exposed and experienced we become in extending compassionate healing presence, the more we are able to witness the cathartic release and feel our companion's relief and return to peace. The more prepared we are to allow ourselves to be pulled through the same experience, the more we can simultaneously transform our own trauma, often with an ease that defies our comprehension.

Over a year later, a series of events unfolded which brought forward an obscure cousin who had been secretly adopted out of the family. As they reconnected, Selene realised that this long lost cousin shared some very similar experiences to her own. They both felt as though they had never really fitted into their birth family. Selene relished the chance to commune with her cousin and explore the similarities between their life paths. Graeme was 15 years older than Selene and was just as sensitive and aware of his emotions as she was. They instantly connected and began to relay details of their individual experiences together. Selene was able to explain how it was for her to lose a younger sibling and Graeme was able to relay how sad and alone he felt as an 'outsider', always knowing that he was adopted. Graeme felt feel a sense of shame and fear worrying that he might be discovered crying and grieving for his birth family! Even though these family members were now meeting for the first time following completely different family upbringings and conditions, it struck them both simultaneously how truly alone they had both felt. They shared the same sense of shame around the depth of sadness that erupted from their hearts whenever they were alone. Selene and Graeme were able to hold each other in so much compassion that they both felt truly witnessed and seen. The love that generously poured in from one another somehow flowed simultaneously through to touch both of their hearts and eliminate any sense of shame that had been residing there. Of course they could both see how natural and normal these deep feelings of sadness were, given the circumstances of their lives.

Our healing presence emanates from a willingness to hold ourselves in compassion, as we recognise that our original goal to witness and acknowledge the suffering of others is at war with another prior commitment - to ignore our most painful moments of emotional suffering. This is a divinely orchestrated paradox and the exposure to this impasse will surface again and again, until we are sufficiently trusting of grace to allow ourselves to surrender and enter into a new perception. There are two paths you can choose from: we can hold ourselves in compassion and permit ourselves to witness our own suffering in the reflected presence of another, or we witness the reflected suffering of another, and likewise receive the same brave acknowledgement which we wish to extend.

Ultimately, I believe our ability to sense and feel the pain in others is a way of preparing us to someday return to witness our own unacknowledged pain, so that it can be freed. We need to remove the false perception that anything that can exist in the emotional realm cannot be felt and transmuted with love. The more experienced we are in offering compassionate presence, the more prepared we are to be witnessed by others. As our experience of giving and receiving compassionate healing presence expands, so too does our ability to sense and know our truth. No matter what we have endured, our pain can burrow a desire to love others so deeply into our hearts - that it becomes the same passageway to our own liberation. Our willingness to love others becomes the gateway to feeling and knowing we too are loved.

## *Healing Guidance:*

1. Write down one moment when you could recognise that **someone else** had endured a difficult experience in life that was able to **match and mirror your own**?

2. Has it been **easier** for you to **witness** the suffering in others, or the suffering within yourself?

3. What **truth** was revealed as you extended **compassionate presence** to someone with a similar experience to your own suffering?

# *Healing Affirmations:*

- *I trust others with their suffering*
- *Suffering refines us all*
- *I witness suffering with deep compassion*
- *Suffering ennobles the human soul*
- *As I look in upon others with love, I see deeper into my own heart*

# Chapter 3

## Wounded Lovers or Healing Union?

*The truth is that Empaths can hide their own needs, fears and trauma from themselves, so that they can make more space to care for others. But eventually, after enough of being 'taken from', we start to allow the unease within us to confirm that we truly do need to receive too.*

*I*f we ignore and deny our true nature as Empaths, we will consistently attract romantic partners who need us to help them to heal. Our capacity to discern the emotional climate, needs and past trauma within others means that we are super attractive to those who need to process their past pain. Empaths who are unaware of their disposition to read others emotionally can unintentionally find themselves engaged in painful, ongoing healing work in their relationship with their partners. These 'Wounded Lovers' who seek and find us can become our sacred teachers, helping us to claim and own the true role we are here to play.

Empaths have such a huge vulnerability around receiving because of past experiences of betrayal, loss and abandonment; we can pretend that 'we don't need anything' and take comfort staying in the 'giving' aspect of our nature. By falling into a pattern of serving and supporting our lovers, we can observe how easily we can help them to progress, improve and heal. But if we don't learn how to cultivate our receptivity, we could miss out on finding a healing union in which we can mutually give and receive in balanced reciprocity.

While it's true that every human soul is in need of healing, there is a clear separation between those who are willing to 'take responsibility' for themselves, and those who are willing to 'rely on others'. Empaths can sometimes be prone to an illusion that if they are loving, supportive and caring enough, then the eyes of their lover will somehow be opened and we will finally be appreciated. But, it doesn't actually work like that! When we get so lost in 'giving', we can fall into the role of 'Saviour' and 'Rescuer'! If our identity is limited to these roles, it will leave no space for our whole truth to be received and embraced. Becoming what our companion needs (in order to receive love) is a fear based strategy that actually keeps us from the truly reciprocal love we yearn for.

Lorraine had a history of falling into relationships with wounded men. Lorraine had been dating George in Sydney for about 9 months; he still held a lot of regret around his former girlfriend, who had broken up with him two years previously. Things seemed to be going well for the pair when George suddenly found out that his mother had sustained an injury after an accidental fall; he needed to return home to Spain immediately to stay by her side while she recovered. His one-way ticket was booked and with only 3 days left together, George mentioned that he wanted to catch up with a few friends and a past girlfriend before his departure. Initially, Lorraine thought she would be fine spending time with her boyfriend's friends and his ex, because she wanted to enjoy as much time by his side as she could in the lead up to his departure. Plans were made to meet at a local restaurant, so that everybody could gather in one location and share a beautiful meal together to farewell George. When Lorraine sat down at the table, she was instantly overwhelmed by a feeling of longing and regret. She couldn't see any clear indication of where this feeling was coming from. She had to breathe deep and concentrate, and by disregarding what she saw before her, she narrowed in on the feelings and she found she could pin-point it. There was definitely an infatuation and longing within George towards his ex-girlfriend. They were simply sitting and talking, but in Lorraine's body, she knew that her boyfriend was still very much in love with his ex-girlfriend and her heart was crushed. Lorraine didn't say anything at the time - how do you hold someone accountable for their unacknowledged feelings?

Lorraine felt incredibly confused by the whole experience. George departed back home to Spain and the longer she was away from him, the more clearly she could see how one-sided their relationship had been. Lorraine broke up with him, deep down she knew she was only a replacement for the woman he truly loved. Lorraine was able to recognise that her overwhelming desire to find love had made her far too willing to accept what was readily available. The rising anger motivated a daring new act; to abstain from men and actually date herself. She was committed to investing the same devotion and care she had previously reserved exclusively for her lovers into her own precious heart.

The truth is that Empaths can hide their own needs, fears and trauma from themselves, so that they can make more space to care for others. But eventually, after enough of being 'taken from', we start to allow the unease within us to confirm that we truly do need to receive too. We need to pay attention to this genuine desire and openly accommodate ourselves if we want to forge a loving union. Empaths can turn the tide on their tendency to over-give by learning how to feel safe in receiving. Being able to recognise that we must find comfort in our own vulnerability allows us to gradually open up.

Lorraine was contact by a teenage crush, Adam; a dear friend from decades earlier. Lorraine had been talking on the phone to Adam for 3 months when he said he wanted to come over from America to New Zealand to visit. When Lorraine picked Adam up from the airport, she could feel how intent and committed he was on marrying her. Lorraine shared *"I was scared, excited and deeply confronted. I decided to speak up and be more honest than ever before. After a long series of disappointing relationships I was committed to being who I really was. I just knew that I needed to speak the truth"*. Sensing Adam's intention to propose, Lorraine quickly spoke up: *"Please don't ask me any important questions today! I don't feel ready to have that conversation."* Adam looked completely shocked. Lorraine and Adam ended up getting engaged 4 months later, and after they were married he confided that he was shocked when Lorraine had said *"No important questions today!"* because he was planning on proposing to her in those moments.

Lorraine had really shifted herself from being 'the Giver', to being both 'the Giver' and 'the Receiver'. Her practice with dear friends had confirmed that when she allowed herself to speak up and share her true feelings, she would be heard and helped. Lorraine did feel vulnerable, but she also felt incredibly loved. She was able to witness first-hand that being willing to co-create in a relationship made the connection far more meaningful and rich for both parties. It was a startling revelation for Lorraine. From the moment that Adam came onto the scene, she decided to do things very differently: she made space for her feelings to be shared, she spoke up when she needed to clarify something and she was willing to cringe in discomfort by revealing her weaknesses. Adam was able to really hear Lorraine and hold her in so much love that when she did share her heart, he could help her to feel safe.

Empaths can open up to a union of healing love in their romantic relationships when they are able to practice becoming more conscious of how they tend to 'perform' in their relationships. We do not need to 'help' others to be worthy of love. We all have weaknesses, vulnerabilities and heartaches from the past that need to be heard and seen with compassion. When we taste the possibility of a healing union, it becomes the benchmark for what we can accept in any relationship. This principle is equally relevant with friendships and business partnerships, mutual reciprocity creates a balanced equation in all relationships. Being able to give and receive is the key to resounding love that amplifies and grows, creating a sense of heaven on earth for all involved.

## *Healing Guidance:*

1. Name one former partner who showed you their wounds, but **refused to heal**?

2. What have you **healed or shifted** since you were with that partner?

3. How can you show yourself **more love and devotion** this month?

# *Healing Affirmations:*

- *It is safe and balanced to both give and receive love*
- *I choose to invest my healing power into my own heart*
- *I am loving myself to attract a partner who can love themselves too*
- *My self-healing attracts a partner who is self-healing*
- *I am worthy of investing my love and devotion into myself first*

# Chapter 4

## Parenting the Parents or Nurturing the Inner Child?

*Empath children can find it confronting to sense feelings within others that do not match the meaning associated with the words they are verbally expressing at the time. Conflicted adults abound, and these Empath children need to be able to hear from adults who share vulnerable, sincere words that are a direct match to their authentic feelings inside.*

*E*mpaths are born predisposed to nurture those around them. Their ability to truly discern genuine needs means that they are keenly aware of the often unspoken needs of the people close to them. If they can sense sadness, they know how to offer comfort and reassurance. If they can sense anger, they know how to create space for honest dialogue. But it's the emotional deficit remaining within the parents that Empaths will commonly seek to fill and counter-balance. As these children are largely unaware of the full extent of their abilities, they can go to great lengths to manoeuvre themselves into the gap and fulfilling the perceived need requirement. If this tendency is not recognised and re-directed, Empath children can lose touch with their own emotional needs as they become fixated in providing for the two people whom they are most reliant upon. True to their nature, Empath children hold no judgment towards their parents' lack of maturity or inability to parent; an Empath (of any age) will simply twist themselves inside out in order to meet the requirements of the moment, whatever that may be.

Empath children believe that everyone thinks and perceives the world the same way that they do. They believe that everyone can honestly discern the world of emotion within themselves, and they expect others to speak honestly about the truth of what is happening. Unfortunately, the majority of adults have been taught to deny the existence of emotion within themselves; instead, they often pretend to feel and behave in ways that fit the expectations of the cultural norms which they have inherited. The established values of their community influence individuals in the ways they think, feel and behave, to conform to expectations of what is deemed 'orderly' and 'constructive' for society.

Empath children can find it confronting to sense feelings within others that do not match the meaning associated with the words they are verbally expressing at the time. Conflicted adults abound, and these Empath children need to be able to hear from adults who share vulnerable, sincere words that are a direct match to their authentic feelings inside. This is how we can support Empath children to feel safe and confident with their perception living in this world – to be able to discern who is lying and who is telling the truth? They can eventually identify the difference between those who are lying consciously and self-deceivers - those who don't even know that they're lying at all! Without the ability to differentiate between these, Empaths are unable to trust themselves to navigate what information they can receive and rely on, and what information they can safely reject and ignore.

Ideally, we are born into families who offer love, support and nurturing guidance to children, providing them with a safe space to learn and grow. Such environments are able to instil a clear sense of 'self-worth' which allows children to feel safe around their 'worthiness to receive' and prepares them for the responsibilities of adulthood. This sense of 'self-worth' allow young people to grow up and become adults who can make loving contributions to their families, communities and career. Having said that, in my experience, no-one leaves their home environment with all of their needs met! There will always be some level of disfunction associated with certain challenges from these formative years and these limitations should be viewed positively, as they can become stepping stones to our personal growth and development later as adults.

Daniella was the second child born into the Martelle family. Mrs Martelle was following the social norm she had been given to get married and raise a family, even though her own mental health denied her from being able to navigate her own internal emotional world. Consequently, Daniella grew up in a home permeated daily by the volatility of her mother. Medication was taken some days, but not others. Finding her mother asleep during the day was common, as was the fighting between her parents that left all three children feeling unsure, uneasy and cautious around their parents.

Daniella learnt to accept her mother's mental health issues and a bond was formed amongst the siblings which meant they could rally together in the event of a downward spiral of their mother's mood. They would take turns 'watching her behaviour' to sound the alarm if attention was required. Daniella learnt to use humour to cheer up her father and her siblings after difficult episodes. There is no capacity for an Empath child to 'reject' their circumstances, no matter how dire; instead that child will reject themselves and believe themselves to be erroneous and worthy of condemnation.

Now a 40 year old, Daniella had her own big family of five to care for. She had accepted that her mother's mental health prevented her from being a reliable source of either support or nourishment, had developed a particular capacity for humour and an incredible ability to turn situations around. These strengths and skills had allowed Daniella to move on from a lot of the confusion and hurt she had experienced in her early years with her mother.

I had been working with Daniella for a few months to support her to feel love and compassion within, when one week she became aware of how tired and low in energy she was feeling. Concerned for her health, she went to visit her doctor, who asked routine health questions to try to find out the cause. After a series of questions he paused and asked if Daniella could be pregnant. She replied "No", as her youngest child now 7 years old, there was no intention of having another child. However, her period was late, so she began considering dates very cautiously.

Within 2 weeks, Daniella had confirmed that she was indeed pregnant, and a depth of discomfort rushed to the surface. Because this was an unintentional pregnancy, she was jolted by the confronting fact that her own judgment towards her mother was now directly relevant to her situation. *"If my mother was mentally ill and didn't actually desire children, then why did she have us?"* was a question she was drawn to reflect upon. The true sentiment of how 'unwanted' Daniella had felt as a child collided with the current reality of her 'unintended pregnancy' with painful agony. Confronted by the coincidence of events that had brought this forgotten or submerged aspect of her childhood to the surface, Daniella was devastated. But together she and I gathered in love, combining our full measure of mercy to shower her with a safe and supportive space which allowed her to tell the truth. Daniella was able to admit that although she initially did not want this pregnancy, nevertheless she was honoured to receive a child. Danielle believed in the sanctity of life and in the pricelessness of every individual. Over the course of the next 2 weeks, Daniella's heart softened, she made alternate plans for her job responsibilities and found all of the necessary items required to receive a baby. With a car seat and bassinet secured, she began to dream of holding another little one in her arms and relished the thought of being able to step back into the mother role with a new-born to support again. Her husband was on board and the day-dreaming of a new life with their little baby began.

The following week, Daniella miscarried. The devastation this time was far more pronounced and profound. The child she had initially rejected, whom she later found herself warmly anticipating and looked forward to welcoming, was no longer on the way. The grief of losing a child is enormous enough, but now Daniella also needed to address the guilt of not joyfully receiving her little one upon first acknowledgement. Empaths have a tendency to disproportionately blame themselves for what has actually happened. Feeling simultaneously guilty and consumed by grief, Daniella verbally expressed to me how devastated she felt to lose a child she had only just received into her heart.

If we find it difficult to hold space for our own error and suffering, accessing supportive compassionate space is essential for us to process and grieve what has happened to us, so that we can see ourselves more clearly. Even as adults, if we can receive a compassionate presence from another, we are able to finally imbue our hearts with a deep sense of trust that despite our errors and human folly, we too are worthy of forgiveness and mercy.

As children, Empaths can invest so much nurture into 'being responsible' for their own parents and families that they fail to experience an understanding of what it is to be truly loved in their own perfect imperfection. Empaths have an amazing capacity to look past the faults and failings of those around them; however, cultivating the ability to see themselves as lovable, worthy and worthwhile is a challenging perspective to acquire! Empath children can grow up to become parents with disproportionate expectations on how they need to live. Expecting the highest from themselves (because they seek to avoid the pain of letting others down) is really a by-product of the desire to avoid any situation where someone could feel the same way they once felt. Falling into deep self-judgement, guilt and shame for their own human error is a common emotional repercussion for someone who has not been assured of their innate worthiness.

# *Healing Guidance:*

1. Recall a moment when **you** needed **nurture**, but gave it to your parent instead?

2. List the family members whom you have either nurtured and cared for as a mother would or provided and protected like a father would, **despite you not being their parent**?

3. Are you ready to redirect the nurturing for your mother and/or the providing for your father into a **sense of permission** that you can truly take care of yourself?

# Healing Affirmations:

- *I forgive myself for parenting my parents*
- *I see myself as worthy of my own parenting*
- *I forgive my parents for not being able to provide for my needs*
- *I choose to adopt myself and invest my love within*
- *I am worthy of my own love and I care first and foremost for myself*

# Chapter 5

## Compulsive Over-giving or Conscious Service?

*We can all too easily accept our role as 'servants' in this life, because we innately value being surrounded by other people whom we can support – we are all too eager to serve, because it allows us to hide from ourselves by prioritising 'their' needs ahead of our own.*

*I*t's tremendously difficult to free ourselves from the binds of compulsive service, because as Empaths, we can be incredibly creative in our ability to find new ways to serve and nurture others, at the cost of serving and nurturing ourselves. Remembering that our emotional experience of every moment is heavily influenced by the emotional experiences of those around us provides the self-compassion to recognise that compulsive service is a stage that every Empath will pass through. Ultimately, influencing and helping others remains compulsive for as long as it takes for us to become aware of the reality of our own needs. We can all too easily accept our role as 'servants' in this life, because we innately value being surrounded by other people whom we can support – we are all too eager to serve, because it allows us to hide from ourselves by prioritising 'their' needs ahead of our own. This repeated exposure to feeling as though other people's feelings are more important than our own conditions us to continually play a role that benefits everyone around us – but not ourselves. Staying in a position of giving perpetuates the lie that we are not worthy of receiving. How long we stay in this position and to what end it affects us personally is our own individual point of power; we are completely free to choose the parameters of this timeline.

Ultimately, we make the shift when the discomfort of needing love from others in return for serving and meeting their needs becomes greater than the discomfort of acknowledging our own needs and being willing to commit to meeting them first (before caring for anyone else). This particular type of emotional discomfort accumulates when we feel 'insignificant and unworthy' of receiving love from others, tipping us towards a willingness to experiment with facing our own neediness and a fear of what we'll lose if we actually show up in deep love and devotion towards ourselves. Facing the possibility of losing the love, acceptance or approval of others who have been trained to rely on our devoted and caring nature is a pivotal fork in the road for every Empath.

Becoming busy is a delicious excuse to not feel our own feelings! Getting lost in helping others can feel like a noble and honourable pursuit; in truth, it's only an escape from needing to compassionately be with ourselves and welcome our own genuine feelings to the surface. Anytime we feel compelled to rush into service, it's crucial to question ourselves and reflect on what we may be trying to avoid by making someone else feel more important than ourselves. It requires us to slow down, to stop caring so much for the needs of others and face ourselves. We can spend years or decades serving the needs of those around us with an imminent and pressing sense of responsibility. But for every other soul that we invest in supporting and helping, we incur a cost to our own progress and healing. It's a transaction we need to evaluate and transcend.

Jennifer is a single mum of one and the owner of three businesses, who is devoted and loyal to her own large extended family. Taking care of those closest to her is what brings Jennifer a huge sense of connection and contribution. But recently, a few unpleasant encounters with friends have confirmed that Jennifer is not as 'taken care of' as she had hoped. Empaths all give without expectation, but nevertheless hope that someday, in some way, they will receive back. Even 10 or 15 years down the track, if a friend were to turn around and really show up to help us in a tricky situation, then all the years of support and service, meals delivered, hours on phone calls and babysitting favours would be well invested.

But Jennifer was becoming increasingly aware that her service was very one-sided, and the amount of time that she was investing in others was consistently not reciprocated. In fact, the people closest to Jennifer had begun to expect and assume that her generosity was never-ending. But it was not; holidays were meant to be a time of relaxation and reprieve, but once operations for her three businesses closed down for the year, a grinding tiredness crept in that took Jennifer by surprise. We were 3 months into our mentoring relationship and Jennifer was becoming aware that her genuine love and care was extending out far beyond the limits of her personal supply. Empaths are often unaware of the true emotional impact of unreciprocated giving, because they are so used to it that it has become embedded in their nature.

Most Empaths have been treated so poorly by those around them for such a prolonged period of time that they simply excuse all of humanity and work all the harder to help everyone, so that they might finally become 'worthy' of attracting caring people into their lives. But Jennifer was increasingly aware of the discontent in her belly and the sense of anger she felt as people continued to take from her without making any reciprocated return. In our mentoring, she began to heed the message of her anger. Jenifer made a decision to start act differently.

Jennifer began saying "No", declining to help some friends and family members. She stopped spending time with friends who were not being kind and supportive in return for Jennifer's help. She even looked at one of her business associates and realised that they were contributing nothing to the growth of the business, so she scaled down her own efforts likewise. This was a daunting and scary task, as it felt incredibly self- indulgent to abstain from helping, because helping was the easiest and most natural thing for Jennifer to do.

Nevertheless, despite her fear and apprehension about this new course of action, Jennifer persisted out of curiosity and came to see how much more energy she had at the end of each day. Slowly and surely, Jennifer used her innate emotional attunement to recognise signals of anger, confirming she had been disrespected. She was able to start acknowledging feelings of sadness that she had been let down and pay attention to the frustration that she was not being considered by people whom she herself had spent a great deal of time considering. Jennifer was scared that she was becoming incredibly selfish by finally putting herself first, but the fact she had more energy, more joy and more happiness shifting into more conscious service all confirmed to her that this new path was right.

Slowly and steadily, Jennifer began to reflect on the rewards she got from investing herself in business and in some of her continuing friendships. Once she stopped compulsively giving and serving, she realised that one business was not making any profit after expenses, and that some friends were actually never there for her. This was a brutal reality for Jennifer to absorb. She used her awareness of this pain to tighten up her boundaries. Over a period of 3 months, Jennifer stopped spending time with any friends who didn't nurture her in return, closed down one unprofitable business and only helped half as many friends and family for free with her home remedy products. This resulted in an increase of energy, joy and financial abundance. By investing her energy and love consciously, Jennifer found the time and energy to grow both of her two remaining businesses. And the results were astounding; clients referred more people to her, they raved about her service and Jennifer had more energy and happiness inside – her whole world had completely changed. There was now no pain in saying "No", increased financial prosperity had lifted her experience of life and Jennifer felt far more appreciated.

Once we start to play with these principles, even if it's only a little, they will bring in new reflections of reality which can confirm how valuable and pivotal these principles are. We never need to apply the ideas 100% from the start – even a seemingly minor 5% or 10% experiment will reveal the value of application. The best way to create powerful change for an Empath is by steadily taking consistent little steps forward. Considering our own needs and being conscious of what we are investing in others, is a supportive way to begin considering how to include ourselves in our conscious service. Questioning ourselves will reveal the changes that are necessary - what do I enjoy? What do I want to give? Am I being appreciated and celebrated for my contribution? Reciprocation is the key to genuine loving service – being honest with ourselves about what we desire and what we truly want to give allows us to re-direct our love and care into that which is truly worthwhile. These endeavours then nourish our own Empath souls and allow us to cultivate and grow our power, while staying invested in those who can truly benefit and reciprocate around us!

## *Healing Guidance:*

1. How many hours have you spent **giving service** this week?

2. How many hours have you spent **serving yourself** this week?

3. What **3 changes** do you need to make to become **more balanced and conscious** about where you give service?

# Healing Affirmations:

- *I am worthy of my own love and care*
- *The more I invest in myself, the more I have to give*
- *Giving to myself creates a fountain of overflowing love inside me*
- *I am the most worthy recipient of my precious love*
- *Caring for myself attracts souls who care for me*

# Chapter 6

## The "Purge and Run" or Sacred Witnessing?

*When strangers approach you time and time again, confiding deeply personal details with you and then fleeing, feeling relieved and lighter, you start to wonder "Why me?" This is a pivotal shift in recognising that you are an Empath – or Natural Healer.*

*A*s we allow the evidence from multiple sources to stack up, it's becoming clear that everyone else can see, sense and feel who we are – except us as Empaths! In this chapter, I'm looking at the influence that strangers have on our self-perception. After considering how our lovers, parents and friends treat us, it has become clearer that we are known for our 'mercy', 'compassion' and 'emotional depth'. In this chapter, we'll dive into the role that strangers – rather than those who know us well - play in confirming our true nature. I believe that we can understand more of who we are by observing those who don't know us interact and respond to our help. When pure strangers are able to discern that you are a soul capable of clearly witnessing their story, we need to start respecting our calling in order to offer our healing presence.

A 'purge and run' is the experience of having a stranger approach you, share their story with you openly, take your response and then leave the scene, never to see you again. It can be incredibly draining to have so much personal information dumped upon you and can easily leave you feeling overwhelmed and confused. After the first couple of times, you can begin to wonder if 'Healer' has been written on your head in magical ink that only the wounded can see? When strangers approach you time and time again, confiding deeply personal details with you and then fleeing, feeling relieved and lighter, you start to wonder "Why me?" This is a pivotal shift in recognising that you are an Empath – or Natural Healer.

What if we were all far more perceptive than we have been led to believe? What if you knew that out of a crowd of 100, which individuals could hear, witness and stay with you in love? It seems impossible in this context, yet time and time again at school, social parties and amongst our daily activities, those who feel burdened and heavy with a load of pain or discomfort are able to recognise us and generate an authentic approach in order to share their story with us. Have you ever been with taxi drivers, hairdressers or have met strangers on the street and have been surprised by how willingly they relay incredibly private or emotional disturbing information with you – speaking casually as though they had known you for your whole life? This chapter is shining a light on the 'Purge and Run' – a phenomenon experienced by all Empaths that involves finding ourselves exposed to incredibly sensitive vulnerable heart shares, which alleviate some emotional burden in others and but can leave us feeling dumped on and drained!

It's important to recall the private suffering that stacks up in our personal lives when we are exposed to the true emotions and vulnerable inner worlds of others. We become very accepting people because we ourselves have felt personally judged and ridiculed by others. Those moments of being rejected, abandoned or misunderstood cultivate a huge amount of compassion and acceptance, because we never want someone else to feel how we have been left to feel sometimes. We'll even be capable of enduring personal discomfort in order to alleviate the burden of another. The problem is that we are so clearly a compassionate presence for so many. What is it about who we are that can so obviously assure others of the safety and care we can offer?

Natalia was a soft spoken art teacher who loved to use vibrant colour and liberal self-expression to support her students in expressing themselves and their true feelings genuinely. In just a few brief words, Natalia was able to usher her students into an almost meditative state of deep calm and reflection, in which their connection to the brush and canvas could transport them to a new world. Natalia was an expert in using creative expression to travel and sojourn in new destinations; her presence was the key to unlocking this same power for her students. Natalia loved to escape to new realities, because her own had been so hard to bear; losing her twin sister at only 8 years old had cast Natalia out-of-phase with real time, as she felt a terrible longing to be with her sister. Natalia found herself exposed to this new and very coarse world of grief and isolation, which few cared to step into and accompany her in. Natalia's parents had lost sight of their living daughter due to the devastation of losing their other child. There was so much grief within the family that Natalia's life developed a sense of hollowness which she could not evade. Not being spoken to very much, being asked to go away and play alone and only very rarely being held in a comforting embrace etched a sense of isolation into her heart. As time went on, Natalia developed the ability to 'disappear' when she did not want social company or conversation and then 'appear' to those with whom she felt a connection. Invariably, when she was present in the company of others, Natalia would happenchance upon an individual who felt particularly lonely or overwhelmed with grief. Somehow the two would be drawn together and Natalia would end up listening to and acknowledging their sad tale, devastating loss or burden of grief to such a degree that her companion would feel lighter and highly relieved afterwards. Natalia would feel grateful that she could offer this compassionate presence to another human being, but she also felt deeply conflicted by the lingering sense of confusion and heaviness in her body. It was usual for her never to see the individuals whom she'd connected with again, or for those she'd helped to only speak to her afterwards on a superficial level.

An enormous sense of isolation is such a prevalent experience for Empaths. As these 'purge and run' experiences mount, they gather together to form a case supporting the idea that we only have worth by becoming 'emotional dumping zones' for others. We use our own physical bodies as places where people can come to freely relieve themselves of their emotional discomfort. The experiences layer up and we reach a level of 'fullness' to the point at which we simply can't bear to allow someone else to divulge any further suffering to us. The feeling that we may sink straight right down to the depths if we are exposed to even one more heart purge begins to take hold. Natalia had been the unwilling witness for school friends, extended family and strangers for so many years that she simply chose to become 'permanently invisible' as a radical act of self-defence. Never wearing make-up, choosing to wear pale muted colours and walking with her head down was the unintentional safety protocol for someone struggling to comprehend their purpose in a world so full of suffering. Natalia was afraid that there was no possible way to remove herself from the stream of suffering that constantly showed up around her, other than to simply fade into the background.

Experiencing an enormous amount of success as her Artist Expression Workshops grew in demand, Natalia wanted to further grow her business and expand with more classes. I was excited to stand by Natalia in our mentoring relationship and guide her on the initial steps, helping her to feel safe in becoming more visible. Revealing herself more clearly would allow her to showcase her skills and communicate her expanding teaching schedule to reach new students in additional locations. Helping others to access the joyful and free explorative space her work had become known for became her personal mission. But suddenly the desire to touch more students was met by a fear of exposing herself to even more opportunities to be 'purged' upon. I love the juxtaposition of our genuine desires colliding with our biggest fears, because we only have two options: to disown our genuine desires (and face the dull grey reality of life without any of our precious dreams fulfilled), or to witness our fears and re-evaluate our response strategy, so we can find new ways of being and to open up to our vulnerability. Natalia agreed that she couldn't deny the knowing that she must expand her Artist Expression Workshops, so it was time for us to re-evaluate her perception of herself that had been forged through repeated 'purge and run' dumps, leaving her feeling fearful, used and puzzled, questioning why so many people would talk to her so openly about their deep personal pain.

Being able to witness my Empath clients' suffering firs
a powerful pattern interrupt as they are able to truly f
ease which washes in when they feel completely safe an... .
Knowing that their past pain can be heard and witnessed by some....
else allows a level of relief in which they suddenly understand the
value of what they had been offering to others for so long. Experiencing 'sacred witnessing' is a transformational experience, when you
can sense and feel that your past pain does not submerge, burden or
damage the listener to any degree. Natalia felt buoyed up in love as
she could freely relay how it really felt to lose her dear twin. *"Having
someone that was so close, so easy to love and so understanding of
me, made life feel completely empty and barren after she left"* Natalia
confided. Together we cried and made ample space for the sentences
of grief and the flow of emotion to come forward, unencumbered and
free. Over a series of appointments, Natalia could feel more space,
more room to breathe deeper and a sense of safety knowing she was
not alone; she was able to imbue her moments with a new sense of spaciousness. Natalia was coming back to life and was feeling real ease
around allowing herself to be; this gave her the courage to become
more confident and visible.

Natalia didn't need to pretend she wasn't here anymore. Over the
next few months she took inspired steps with a new photography
shoot, organising client testimonials and new venue locations for her
events. She decided to create a sharing space in her Artist Expression
Workshop in which all attendees could be heard for 5minutes apiece.
Consciously creating an allowance for her class to share their truth
and receive the experience of being witnessed by all of those present
was a very intentional act of self-acceptance. The sacred witnessing
that Natalia had been encumbered with across her whole life now
became an intentional offering in her workshop experience. Cultivating a culture of love, acceptance and tolerance allowed Natalia's
students to themselves practice listening, giving and receiving in

sacred witnessing, with remarkable results. From that time forward, few strangers sprang their life story upon her. As Natalia created conscious space to truly hear and witness those she chose to invest her abilities in, the surprise and discomfort of the 'purge and run' all but vanished from her life.

When we shift into finding acknowledged, acceptable ways to share our presence, we remove the shame and fear around our purpose as Empaths. When strangers repeatedly utilise your natural gifts to alleviate themselves of emotional discomfort and inner turmoil, you are able to confirm the natural ability that you do have. The 'purge and run' experience is a behaviour laden with shame; the shame we feel around our hidden pain, the shame we feel knowing we need to express it and the shame of not having anyone who can truly hear us in our lives. I helped Natalia to understand that just because she could hear suffering, she didn't need to accept it everywhere she went. Crafting a conscious outlet in which she could establish safe boundaries and acceptable parameters that could be agreed upon socially gave birth to an elevated experience within her Artist Expression Workshops. Now, Natalia not only prospers from her exceptional ability to witness, but knows that no matter what happens in life, she is supported by individuals close to her who will hear her, love her and receive her at any time she feels vulnerable or overwhelmed.

## *Healing Guidance:*

1. Name the **feeling/s present** when you experienced the first 'purge and run' that you can remember?

2. What have you made the tendency for others to purge and confide such intimate details with you **mean about yourself**?

3. Do you still want to **invite** others to confide deeply intimate information in you, or do you **choose** to be ready to **no longer invite** this behaviour into your life?

# *Healing Affirmations:*

- *Those near me can sense my truth*
- *I am trustworthy and compassionate*
- *I am a safe space for others*
- *I honour my natural healing presence*
- *I allow myself to turn away from emotionally loaded situations*

# Chapter 7

# Self-Pity or
# Self-Advocacy?

*While the circumstances and characters within the stories of others are different to ours, the pain at the centre of their hearts reflects our own.*

*E*mpaths despise self-pity - we are so keenly aware of the suffering of so many that any self-indulgence invested in pitying one's own personal plight is met with harsh judgement. This is actually what causes us to stay in denial regarding our own self-care for so long. Any dip in our mood or inclination to bemoan our plight is rejected and is quickly replaced by some more 'worthy' mission to help others who are 'suffering more than us'. Attempting to minimise our own suffering by exposing ourselves to something or someone more 'worthy' of our care and concern is a destructive habit that can only wear us down and dramatically deplete our reserves. Knowing exactly how everyone is suffering cements our acceptance of the truth that everyone is facing something that is close to unbearable for them personally. This perspective can leave little room for compassion for our own self-pity – because if everyone is suffering, why should we be allowed to moan or complain about our own individual circumstances?

Pain is intended to attract our attention, and it has a provocative way of stealing our focus on the external world, instead drawing us within to confront our private and personal suffering. This is the point at which we can begin to reflect on what our own experience of life has been, when previously all we could witness and consider were the private challenges of everyone else. Eventually, our own pain becomes so pronounced that it demands our attention. Therefore every other individual we have been called to witness ultimately offers us a reflective insight into our own pain. Our compassion and care for everyone else ultimately generates an ability to perceive our own self-pity – because if they have truly suffered (and they have), then we can finally acknowledge that we have suffered too. While the circumstances and characters within the stories of others are different to ours, the pain at the centre of their hearts reflects our own. Perpetually witnessing the hardship of others and offering love and care through compassion means that we inevitably reach the conclusion that our personal challenges have been 'too much'. We crave and yearn for some angelic individual who can perform the sacred function which we have rendered to so many others – a gentle compassionate witness to hold us in mercy and hear us with real love.

In my experience, it's very common for the acquisition of such mercy and compassion to prove almost unobtainable. Ultimately, the lack of this rare gift then illuminates its true value and we can take another big step deeper into self-acknowledgement. Our own personal crisis becomes a tipping point for this shift toward introspection. Rather than perpetually helping everyone else, we instead become more willing and develop the ability to actually show up and help ourselves. It's as though we are truly verifying the value of compassionate presence and vetting its true power by being willing to invest it in ourselves. Once we are able to take our own medicine, we're transported to heightened awareness that it is our responsibility as adults to advocate for ourselves.

Gabrielle had always felt highly sensitive; her ability to tune into the energy and emotion of people and places meant that she alone was hyper-aware of information that those around her were oblivious to. Whilst her family were caring and loving, her empathy and sensitivity was not fully understood, acknowledged or supported. She quickly learnt that in order to receive love in her family, she had to 'get on with it' and was led to denial of the intensity of these emotions.

Without the ability to explain to others what she was sensing, and with them unable to verify her unique and deeper perspective on life, Gabrielle's 'over the top' behaviour was sometimes seen as 'needy' and 'dramatic', when in fact being a small child exposed to the full gamut of human dysfunction, invisible suffering and generational wounding was overwhelming and terrorising for this small Empath child. Being forced to not only face the intensity of the whole wide world around her but do so alone, without any deep emotional support or compassion, forced Gabrielle into the only self-preservation strategy she knew: denial. If Gabrielle could pretend that she wasn't overwhelmed, sad or scared, then she would fit in and feel safe. To a level of success, Gabrielle found there was a thin veneer of safety to be found behind her flimsy fortress of denial. Pretending that everything was okay helped her to fit in, but did nothing to address or alleviate the truth of how challenging life felt for her sometimes.

Fast forward some three decades and Gabrielle had hired me for mentoring. Finding a kindred Empath who is willing to openly speak about their feelings, offer authentic emotional experiences and share genuine personal challenges can feel like a breath of fresh air. Finally, in me, Gabrielle had found someone who could hear her with compassion and reflect back an understanding of her view which allowed her to normalise what she had been encumbered to carry alone for so long. I encouraged Gabrielle to be open to speaking about her gifts and abilities and saw that she was really able to blossom by accepting her true nature; finally, she found a sense of safety in being who she was in the world. Cultivating new boundaries and new behaviours to support her nature allowed Gabrielle to find a sense of ease and weightlessness in accommodating herself. Now actively creating a life that supported her, Gabrielle began crafting a lifestyle that felt nourishing and was able to find a way of being that gave her real joy.

Unfortunately, though, all of this progress began to highlight a huge reservoir of self-pity within Gabrielle. The external circumstances of her life began to improve so significantly that it created a construct which confirmed how deeply hurt and disappointed Gabrielle had been in the past - cue the entrance of unavoidable self-pity! Isn't it funny that it's often when life starts to improve that we find it far easier to actually admit how terrible things have been for us in the past? Progress creates a new level of safety for us to acknowledge the unspoken suffering which has accumulated over a lifetime. I knew that Gabrielle would need support to find the grace to actually admit to how difficult things had been for her. The new age movement often preaches an idea around the law of attraction, insinuating that 'the more we speak about something – the more we will attract it into our lives'. This one concept has been an unintentional justification for many to stay in denial and never admit to their own personal hurt or the tragedy within themselves. The outcome of this can result in a feedback loop whereby no matter how much our lives progress or improve, we can end up staying subconsciously connected to the unacknowledged trauma and suffering in our past. We can thus believe that external progress is a façade that can never change how we truly feel within. Huge endeavours such as weight loss, building a business or buying our dream home can take years to achieve – but when our goals are finally achieved but don't make us feel 'entirely happy', we can give up and return to our previous status quo in order to recover from the feelings of disappointment and powerlessness stemming from the belief that we don't know how to change our inner emotional landscape.

So, just for a moment, I want to advocate for us to actually acknowledge the truth of our past suffering and observe how, when it can be witnessed with compassion, it can be transformed and dissolved. It's only when something is acknowledged and known to us that it can be accepted, integrated and resolved. By telling the truth that parts of our past experiences were excruciatingly painful, we are honouring the person we were then and witnessing them – that what they felt, perceived and endured was indeed excruciatingly painful. This admission alone can lift and dissipate the damage of what we passed through. Truly the most excruciating suffering of all is to believe that our personal pain is insignificant, unworthy or 'made up'. The idea that our pain or suffering is illegitimate or fake is one of the core reasons why people don't confide or share their personal struggles. The judgement that what we are finding incredibly difficult is actually 'nothing at all' – is such a desecration that we often suffer alone is silence in order to save ourselves from the greater pain of having our experience dismissed by someone else. Actually acknowledging how difficult things have been for us, how unloved we had felt or how excruciating some moments were for us means that at least someone recognises the truth of what we have passed through, even if that someone is just us ourselves, through the process of self-acknowledgement. When we focus on creating an honest relationship with ourselves, we can begin to resolve our previous denial (and that of others) with compassionate healing presence.

Gabrielle began to recognise how incredibly alone she had felt and how isolating it had been to have felt so different to those around her. It was not her fault that she was perceived in this way, but it was time for her to find how to hold herself in love and acknowledge how deep her personal despair actually had been. Together, we held Gabrielle in compassion and allowed her to start drawing up the sad and difficult moments she had experienced, so that she could witness and observe herself with genuine love. Gabrielle was brave enough to actually face her past pain and allow it to be released and to vanish from her body. The sensation of transformation is an effervescent cascade of tingles and bubbles, with heavy and dark experiences becoming light and clear. The sense of liberation and power this gave Gabrielle was astonishing; it was as though she realised that she always had a truly loving supporter on hand at every moment. Someone who could see her, love her and stay with her in compassionate witness. It was like a whole new world.

When we feel the warmth and care created from compassionately witnessing ourselves, our tolerance for being disrespected drops rapidly. There is no way in which we are going to permit anyone else to mistreat, deceive or disrespect us when we have a compassionate witness within us at all times. Some months after her breakthrough, Gabrielle was struck by the repetitive disrespect that was surfacing in her personal life. Being criticised by people around her and treated disrespectfully by colleagues – the onslaught was more apparent and harder to tolerate than ever before. It was because when Gabrielle had been continually speaking to herself unkindly, the external disrespect had largely gone unnoticed; it was just an acceptable part of the scenery to receive a continuum of cruelty. While this behaviour had once been accepted and tolerated, it was now standing out sorely and was absolutely unacceptable to Gabrielle. She was now able to walk away from disrespect and cruel taunts, if she was being treated unkindly; she would simply remove and isolate herself until she had recovered. But we needed to equip Gabrielle with more authentic behavioural responses so that she could find a more suitable way to address a full range of experiences. I introduced the principle of self-advocacy, and being able to say *"I don't like being spoken to like that"*, *"It's not OK for you to be so rude to me"* and *"I will not accept being treated like this"*. Empaths initially cringe at the idea of self-advocacy and fear that by speaking up for ourselves, we will appear 'mean', 'uncaring' or 'demanding' – but ultimately, once we can witness our own pain with compassion, we become intolerant of mistreatment and this is a powerful and pivotal shift for our progress. Advocating for ourselves is actually taking a stand for the whole human race - if we cannot speak up and address behaviour which disrespects us, then we are confirming that others like us should likewise stay silent and accept mistreatment. Gabrielle was scared to start speaking up, but she knew the pain of feeling disappointed in herself was necessary for this radical shift.

While at work one day, towards the end of her shift, a co-worker began to question Gabrielle regarding how a task had been completed. Gabrielle needed to complete her current task so replied, *"I'll just finish this task and then I'll come and see what you mean"*, to which her colleague began to raise her voice and assert that Gabrielle didn't know what she was doing and that the quality of her work was unacceptable. Gabrielle had halted her task at this point, confronted by the antagonism being presented to her by this colleague. Gabrielle calmly raised her hand and said *"I will not accept being yelled at, even if I have made a mistake"*. Her colleague continued to raise her voice, so Gabrielle got up and walked straight to the owner's office to relay what had happened. She said *"I need you to know that Sally's behaviour is unacceptable. She can't yell at me and be demeaning and think it's acceptable to correct my mistake in this manner. I'm leaving work now, and I want you to go and speak with Sally and resolve this"*. Gabrielle left the premises and drove home feeling very upset. However, she was able to hold herself in so much love and offer herself compassion and sanctuary, in which she could hold her own feelings in care and kindness. Later that night, she called the owner to discuss what has happened, now that she felt centred again. The owner, Rose, was able to confirm that she had spoken to Sally, agreed that speaking to another staff member in that way was unacceptable and apologised for what had happened. The next day there was a team meeting, at which Sally was able to publicly apologise to Gabrielle and new conditions for behaviour were outlined and clarified.

Gabrielle now knew what it was like to self-advocate and what a powerful tool this can offer us. When we speak up and clarify what is not acceptable for us, we open ourselves to being supported and respected more by others. Gabrielle now giggles when acknowledging that her willingness to honour her own suffering has brought her a greater sense of being loved than she has ever previously known. This feeling of truly being loved and supported to live from her truth has birthed a series of "boundary infringement notices"! Gabrielle is now so clear on what behaviour is and isn't acceptable to her (which she recognised by reviewing her past pain and using those experiences to clarify her personal boundaries) that she can clearly and easily speak up when she recognises that something is outside of her personal tolerance limitations.

We can stay choose to 'stay small' and refuse to give ourselves what we desire because of the emotional ramifications of what it will take for us to truly speak up and be heard. Our own unprocessed grief can build up and act as a barrier standing in the way of our maturity to blossom. Trying to ignore and deny the intensity of our own suffering is a futile mission that requires a huge amount of energy to keep hidden and sunk from our conscious awareness. In this space, we unknowingly hold ourselves back from taking the risks which will bring us a great sense of personal safety and belonging in our lives. Being able to compassionately view ourselves as the witnesses of all of humanity allows us to comprehend why it was so difficult to acknowledge our own suffering. Maybe by keeping it hidden from ourselves we could minimise the true expansiveness of pain - creating a container of sorts that could minimise the fallout, even if it is a self-fabricated illusion? Suffering is certainly no respecter of persons and we all know how prevalent it is across all cultures and societies around the planet and across all time periods. Our desire to alleviate the suffering of others is what drives us to stay and be present to the truth within, by cultivating incredible acceptance, endurance and patience for others. We can only claim our full capacity to truly transform the suffering of others by being willing and prepared to acknowledge and accept our own.

# Healing Guidance:

1. It's time to allow yourself to **review your suffering** and permit a sacred moaning and acknowledgement of the hardship you have known. Dedicate one night to **truly expressing your dismay, hurt and disappointment** around an aspect you have never let yourself verbally express before.

2. Explore being able to **witness yourself with compassion**; observe how it feels to hold yourself in merciful kindness and compassion. Write down what you feel, sense and experience from this **sacred self-investment**.

3. What do you need to **speak up and self-advocate** for in your life this month? Record the one thing you most need yourself to address and devote the month ahead to **honouring and fulfilling this need** for yourself.

# *Healing Affirmations:*

- *I freely permit myself to complain and acknowledge my suffering*
- *Permission to moan harnesses anger and transforms it into power for change*
- *I accept the injustice and imperfection of life; I speak up to advocate for myself*
- *Complaining holds the potential for activism and advocacy*
- *Acknowledging my suffering frees it from my being*

# Chapter 8

## Deepening Dependency or Selfless Self-Devotion?

*When we realise we have lived in 'needs providing' roles, there is a huge sense of loss in recognising what we did not ourselves receive. The grief can seem somewhat intellectually illegitimate, as we realise that we are mourning the loss of something that was never given in the first place.*

ecause of our innate ability to discern the needs and others, it's common for Empaths to find other people to be quite reliant and dependent upon them. Our master ability to support others can become overly relied upon, leading to co-dependency. As an Empath stays in the core 'needs providing' position, they can easily attract others who require their needs to be fulfilled. Co-dependency is having one person in the 'needs providing' position and another person in the 'needs receiving' position. By becoming addicted to this role, we are perpetually ignore our own needs by constantly being distracted by the task of fulfilling the needs of others.

All Empaths have experienced co-dependency at one point in their lives. Any compulsive behaviour that we need to perpetuate - whether staying reliant upon others or allowing others to be reliant on us - indicates our inability to perceive, identify and provide for our own core needs. Co-dependency is a place that we all end up in when we have not had our own core needs perceived and met as young children. There are two response strategies to not having our needs fulfilled: we either prioritise everybody else's needs over our own and make it a soul preoccupation to support others, or we become dependent on other people to fulfil our needs, never realising our own power to do this for ourselves.

Many of us will swing between both of these patterns interchangeably throughout the years, and often it can be the pain of having others completely reliant on us that causes us to become completely self-focused. If we do withdraw from social relationships, wanting to abstain from providing for the needs of others, we can isolate ourselves and experienced deep loneliness as a consequence. Often in our solitude if we are still unable to perceive our needs, a great sense of anguish and suffering will develop that we experience as a consequence of realising that our relationship with ourselves is at the heart of our challenge.

Beatrice was the first born into the family, and despite their good intentions, her parents' own unmet needs from their upbringings prevented them from being able to truly recognise what their daughter needed. Beatrice was a wise and clever child, who recognised her parents' needs early on; she patiently fell into the role of nurturing her parents in the hope that they would fully receive her and love her in return at some point in the future.

When another child came into the family, the dynamic changed. Born when Beatrice was 5 years old, her brother Tom had cerebral palsy and would require care and support for the duration of his life. Ill-equipped to fully handle the challenges of providing for their son's special needs, it was Beatrice who stepped in to assist her parents, despite her young age. She became a reliable nurturing figure for them all. Over the years, Beatrice and Tom's parents were unable to support each other, as their father was struggling with alcoholism and their mother was unable to acknowledge any of her own suffering and so simply stayed in denial. This void of responsible parenting left Beatrice in the position of having to care for her brother on a daily basis after school. She adopted the role of main carer in the absence of her parents, even though she was only a child herself.

Empath children are wise beyond their years, as their abilities allow them to naturally discern needs. This often means that they fulfil 'care' roles within families, which earns them quite a lot of self-respect, as they can clearly see that their service is so deeply required; this subconsciously imparts a great self of self-importance to the Empath child. Beatrice's mother was always so caught up in the tragedy of her own life and the difficulty of her own situation that she couldn't see that she was placing an extraordinary burden on the shoulders of her daughter. Beatrice was so capable that she didn't complain and delivered years of service in terms of support-ing her entire family.

Beatrice reached out to me wanting support to heal the past and trans-form the relationship she had with her parents. Now married, Beatrice was the mother of three children. It had become obvious to Beatrice as she observed her own children that she had never had the opportu-nity to be a child herself, or to feel safe having her own needs met and provided for. Beatrice felt torn between her old life, with the hardship of needing to care for her disabled brother, and the reality of how carefree, innocent but needy her own children were in her present life. Once again Beatrice was in a position of needing to fulfil the needs of others, but this time around she could appreciate the contrast in circumstances: that her own children legitimately needed her nurture, service and care, while her own childhood was filled unfairly with the responsibility of caring for both her own parents and disabled brother.

When we realise we have lived in 'needs providing' roles, there is a huge sense of loss in recognising what we did not ourselves receive. The grief can seem somewhat intellectually illegitimate, as we realise that we are mourning the loss of something that was never given in the first place. Nevertheless, Beatrice could clearly see that her chil-dren were worthy and deserving of nurture, whilst she had never been able to receive this for herself. Now, as an adult, she needed to allow herself to grieve the innocence and carefree joy of childhood that was never provided for her. She had instead been given a burden of care, in which she lost herself in an overwhelming attempt to fulfil the needs of others.

Together, Beatrice and I were able to truly mourn and grieve the truth that she had not be able to innocently perceive life through the eyes of a child – her sense of responsibility had started early, but now it was finally her time to erect clear boundaries around what and whom she was responsible to care for, and what was no longer her responsibility. All of her relationships fell into question as Beatrice was able to recognise that in every partnership that she had formed, she was in a 'need providing' position. It was easy for Beatrice to lose herself in meeting the needs of others, because she was able to reassure and confirm to herself how valuable and needed she was. The glimmer of appreciation she received from others was sufficient to provide such a sense of satisfaction that she almost couldn't get enough of it! Never being supported to stay in the vulnerable receiving position meant that Beatrice didn't know how to safely open to others. Her weak capacity for receptivity would take time and practice for her to learn how to abstain from caring for anyone else, while she learned instead how to tune in and perceive her own needs and find ways to meet them. This shift involves traversing the deepest sense of shame at even having needs and the sheer terror of discovering how 'selfish' Beatrice might be to actually require anything, let alone acknowledging the desire to finally meet those sacred needs and actually receive from herself.

Nevertheless, Beatrice was committed to training herself to discern when she was 'fulfilling the needs of others' and find how to balance that with a healthy self-regard and self-respect, ensuring that she also fulfilled her own needs. This was a process of re-centring, in which Beatrice could begin to perceive her own innate value. The more she was able to tune in to herself and identify her own needs and fulfil them, the more conscious she became when others were only seeking to have their needs fulfilled. As a result, Beatrice was able to truly feel a sense of calm and safety within herself, knowing she could bask in a deep sense of self-trust that her needs were also worthy and that she was committed to fulfilling them. As a consequence, Beatrice was able to open up to her husband more; she also found the strength to be vulnerable and share what she needed with her friends. Opening up to receive support felt strange and uncomfortable at first - having been seen as 'so capable' for so long - but over time, Beatrice could feel how nourishing and healing it was to permit herself to receive from those she trusted and whom she knew could honour her.

Unfortunately, her parents did not like Beatrice's new self-preserving position and they continued to question and attack her new view on self-protection, whilst constantly reaching out for money, support or food. As outlined previously, every Empath must go through the process of learning how to discern how emotionally healthy our parents are and gauge their capacity to actually show us respect and adjust to our new self-supportive stance in life.

Every one of us truly desires to be loved, supported and acknowledge by our parents. Beatrice found it incredibly hard to hear her parents call her 'selfish' after she adjusted her boundaries. Despite all of her years of service, her parents were unable to recognise their error of relying so heavily upon a child. They were personally offended that Beatrice was withdrawing the generosity that she had provided for nearly three decades. Having support when re-negotiating our core relationships is crucial, because deep connections can have a strong history that we can easily be pulled back into. Saying "No" to her father came easy at times, but in other moments Beatrice would find her ability to sense his pain unbearable and find his requests for money impossible to deny; that's when it was easy to fall back into a 'needs providing' role once again. But each time that she would fulfil her father's needs and placate him, Beatrice would be required to face her own self-imposed injury. Becoming conscious of this trade-off and her own resulting sadness and hurt from inside helped Beatrice to know when she had dishonoured herself. It was the pain in her belly that she would have to face by prioritising anyone else above herself that eventually led Beatrice home to her truth. The more we invest in ourselves, and find how to perceive our own needs and to fulfil them, the more clearly we can discern the intentions of others. As our own needs are fulfilled from within, we can transform our current friendships and see how they can become more balanced, because healthy relationships are based on mutual reciprocity. This opens us up to attract more supportive individuals into our lives and slowly, over time, the temptation to ignore ourselves and invest everything we have into others becomes only a distant memory.

Our emotions hold the key to knowing our true needs, as we learn how to breathe into our bodies and become discerning and conscious of the emotions residing with us - we become capable of conscious self-devotion. We all have the power to identify what we need and to draw on our innate ability to provide for ourselves, as well as being able to reach out to those we love and trust. This realisation can often give birth to the fear that if we truly provide for our own needs, we will have no need for any relationships at all! And while it may cause a sacred swinging of the pendulum for some time, eventually we most certainly do reach a safe place within, where we yearn to give and receive in a balanced, healthy way, in relationships with other conscious caring individuals who are happy to be in a supportive relationship with us.

# *Healing Guidance:*

1. Name one person who **depended on you** (or someone you became dependent upon)?

2. When did you start to rely on **yourself** to fulfil your own **core needs**?

3. Where in your life can you become more **devoted and committed** to yourself?

# *Healing Affirmations:*

- *I am safe and supported to receive*
- *My needs are worth acknowledging*
- *All of humanity has needs and I am safe to acknowledge mine*
- *As I give to myself, I can share more with others*
- *Giving and receiving in equal measure is the sign of a healthy relationship*

# Chapter 9

# Replicating Shadow or Radiating Light?

*Shadow is what remains within that is left unseen, unacknowledged and unlit. It's our life path to bring light to illuminate the areas within ourselves that have not previously been seen by past generations.*

*B*eing so sensitive to the secret realities hidden within the bodies of those around us, Empaths are susceptible to absorbing the perspectives of others; both those said and those unspoken. All trauma is inherited - it is passed on through our intuitive awareness of one another's perception. Our ability to perceive ourselves and our truth is influenced by the ability of those around us to perceive their own truth. As we absorb the perceptions of ourselves through the views of others who have likewise been shown incorrect perceptions of themselves, we are caught in a place where we must all pass through and disregard illusion, in order to return to our pure inner knowing.

Shadow is what remains within that is left unseen, unacknowledged and unlit. It's our life path to bring light to illuminate the areas within ourselves that have not previously been seen by past generations. So truly facing ourselves necessarily involves facing the parts within our parents that they themselves were not able to view in conscious light. It can be tempting to shift into judgment, as we connect some of our own pain with the unconscious actions of our parents, their parents and their parents still. Nevertheless, compassion offers us a softer view, in which we can recognise that our own choice to replicate shadow came purely because we didn't know any better. The key to truly being able to see what needs to be forgiven and illuminated is to first establish a stance of pure mercy.

It's only through merciful kindness that we can turn away from the tendency to fall into judgement and simply witness what 'is'. All of our shadow compulsive tendencies are just loops of judgement. As the adage goes: "We can't get enough of what we don't need" - and there can never be enough money spent shopping to feel better, enough deprivation to make us worthy of love, or enough self-loathing to cover up our fear of truly knowing ourselves. What we do need is a soft place in which we can explore our perception of ourselves in the face of love and compassion.

Cindi was seeking a Mentor to guide her deeper into her truth and true nature, someone who had the ability to see past the self-deception that Cindi knew was her own way of protecting herself. When we met, we instantly felt a connection and both recognised that our combined mercy would create profound synergy.

Together we held the commitment to hold Cindi in love, as she found her own courage and the bravery to see into herself and illuminate what was still hidden in shadow. A recovered bulimic, Cindi had already come so far in healing her tendency to deny herself nourishment and get so lost in food and body judgement that she could evade the real hurt this behaviour was set up to cloak. Cindi had certainly transformed her thinking, emotional awareness and self-perception to such a success that her frame stood strong and her beauty radiated through. However, there was still a lingering irritant that would stir up violent confusion, temptation for self-denial in different forms and an innate distrust of self from time to time. One day, Cindi was relaying to me a pivotal experience from her past, a special time when she was preparing for a dance recital. Contemporary ballet was an outlet for Cindi when she was growing up; it gave her joy to twirl and glide, utilising her strong frame to craft beautiful movement. The self-denial of food had already begun years earlier, but on this occasion, a virus had left Cindi weak and unable to hold down any meals for 2 weeks. Whilst she had rested in bed and allowed herself to sleep and drift in and out of consciousness, Cindi was now feeling better and more able to return to regular meals. On this day from her memory, it was four weeks before her annual dance recital, the pivotal showcase that she had already worked hard towards for the previous 9 months. She went to the bathroom to change into her performance attire, only to find that it was now visibly loose when it had been perfectly fitted just weeks before. Cindi was taking in the sight of her gaunt frame in the bathroom mirror when her mother came in and saw her.

*"Wow, you look beautiful Cindi! It's only 4 weeks until the dance recital - I want you to promise me that you won't regain any of the weight you have lost before the debut night!"* Receiving this acknowledgement and praise from her mother felt so alluring and desirable... Cindi wanted nothing more than for her mother to approve of and celebrate her. That single comment from her mother resonated so strongly that Cindi continued to struggle with anorexia for the following 11 years.

Together, Cindi and I were able to really witness how damaging it had been for Cindi to have been celebrated for her sickness; a 2 week period of physical starvation whilst ill had led to a weight loss that was given approbation and encouragement. To be complimented for ill health and encouraged not to eat, in order to secure recognition and approval, proved horribly alluring. Cindi then allowed herself to perpetuate the denial of food and nourishment so that her mother would continue to be happy and to love her. It was obvious to Cindi that her lovability, attractiveness and worth were dependent upon how thin she was. Together we held both Cindi and her mother in compassion, while recognising how poisonous this experience had been for them both. Together we clarified the real message Cindi interpreted from her mother's comments: *"Your illness and sickness was valuable because it has made you more thin, and the more you deny yourself food – the more worthy of praise, acceptance and adoration you will be. Your worth to me is entirely dependent on your willingness to act, behave and become the person I believe you should be, in order to receive my love."* The combination of our mutual compassion was able to shed light on this message and Cindi was able to cry and mourn the mistake she had made in allowing her mother to influence her in such a destructive way.

Once Cindi could recognise how unsupportive these remarks had been, she could allow them to wash through her and leave her system. Then the true state of Cindi's mother's heart became obvious and alarming - here was a woman who was lost in the idea that she only had value based on how she looked and how thin she was. Cindi's mother had unknowingly repeated the shadow that she was shown and then passed on this perception to her own daughter. Cindi's mother had not acknowledged how destructive and hurtful these ideas had been for herself in her own life - the preoccupation with her weight, what she looked like, and how she could obsess over food and appearance gave her the ability to avoid herself and her truth. When we buy into the idea that we are nothing more than the shell of a body we inhabit, we can become so lost and fixated on controlling the parameters of our appearance so that we can avoid the truth of who we truly are inside.

Cindi was able to effortlessly forgive herself, for unknowingly taking in such toxic and harmful ideas. She found a new softness within, which allowed her to absolutely forgive her mother. From that moment, under the brilliance of shadow illuminated, Cindi was able to consciously recognise that only her opinion of herself truly counted as significant. She was free to disregard the burden of needing the approval of others and fully land into herself. It would now be her own ability to honestly face her own thoughts, feelings and perceptions of herself that could guide and navigate Cindi into an even more nurturing and loving relationship with herself, her truth and her relationship to food and her body.

We are the only ones who can bravely face the illusions that we have inherited and transform them under the conscious light of truth. As we transform our own internal perceptions of ourselves, we are able to clarify our ability to perceive those around us. Honouring the truth of ourselves enables us to likewise honour and respect the truths of those who surround us. Rather than repeating this shadow now and disseminating any ideas that our worthiness is found only in our appearance, we free ourselves to radiate a light that likewise permits the truth of others to shine freely, unencumbered by our judgement.

## *Healing Guidance:*

1. Name one **shadow pattern** you have been shown in your life?

2. What is the **truth that you can perceive** separate from this shadow now?

3. Who can you now **forgive** that has passed on a shadow pattern to you?

# *Healing Affirmations:*

- *Every part I judge in others, also exists in me*
- *Forgiveness frees the shadow self*
- *All shadow is merely repressed light*
- *Removing the shame from parts I have judged, allows them to shine in truth*
- *I allow myself to embody my brilliant light*

# Chapter 10

## Abuse of Authority or Self-Authorisation?

*By authorising and respecting our own guidance as the most reliable and attuned information regarding our situation, we allow ourselves to discern whom we can actually trust and to explore how we can help our own situation.*

*W*e are born into a paradigm which states that people with a certain level of experience, expertise, authority or qualification are supremely capable of solving our personal problems. We are taught to revere those with certain badges and credentials, and recognise these individuals as worthy of our admiration and compliance. The idea that someone bigger, older and wiser can save us from our personal pain is a common human ideal we can all subscribe to. Wanting to attain new insights to help us escape personal pain or challenging circumstances is the basis of both aspiration and delusion! The idea that there are people outside of you who perfectly know what is right for you, who are more credible than your own inner guidance is a fallacy. As experiences accumulate, we also accumulate alarming confirmation that not all experts are genuine, not all professionals have our best interests at heart and not everyone we have been taught to look up to will deliver the desired results we've been led to expect they'll offer. Learning to respect and pay attention to the subtle promptings, internal guidance and knowing within us is a far more effective and positive way in which we can support ourselves to discern what is actually required. By authorising and respecting our own guidance as the most reliable and attuned information regarding our situation, we allow ourselves to discern whom we can actually trust and to explore how we can help our own situation.

Janet's father left the family home when she was only four years old. He came back to visit Janet for a few weekends, but within a year or so he had moved away to another country. He had always been quiet temperamental and unpredictable, so having him out of the family home actually calmed everyone's lives, but even while Janet was young she was mindful of the challenges her brothers were facing due to their dad having gone away. Janet's mother had so much happening personally with increased responsibility for the family that she wasn't able to see how much her youngest child was often overwhelmed and unsure.

Janet became an advocate for others. Friends and cousins who were picked on had to deal with Janet. She wasn't going to leave anyone else feeling alone and unsupported - Janet would jump into a fight easily in order to defend and protect those she cared for. Janet didn't know how to interpret all of the feelings she could sense within herself - she didn't even know what to say if she did speak up and ask for help - she just became somebody who showed up and stepped in to practically protect and care for anyone that she could see needing help; at least she could be there for other people, even if no one was really there for her.

Everyone in the family knew that Janet had information that no one else was privy to. From the time she was little, she would innocently speak up and reveal small phrases, and special words that no one had verbalised to her; her insight came from her innate knowing and premonitions. Janet was right so often that it was confronting for everyone else. Her truth speaking ways were feared and dismissed in this family; how on earth could she know what she was talking about? If Janet spoke up, her family would make her 'wrong'. No matter how truthful, self-evident or recognisable it was that she was telling the truth, her gift and her willingness to vocalise her insights were an inconvenience to everyone else. Janet was repeatedly told in no uncertain terms to stay quiet!

She became more involved in the housekeeping and cooking, so that she could apply herself to something concrete as a way of distracting herself from the disconnect that was growing. Pity towards Janet's brothers was beginning to mount; *"I feel so sad for Steve and Robbie that they have lost their Dad!"* their mother would share with friends.

*"Janet, can you make the boys a smoothie before they go to bed?"* their mother would shout from the lounge room after dinner. *"And make sure you clean up after yourself please? I don't want to wake up to a messy kitchen, thank you very much!"*

*"Yes Mum, smoothies coming up!"* Janet would try to reply in a chirpy tone. The family climate continued to degrade month by month and year by year as the unprocessed grief of losing their father turned into a deep sense of sympathy toward Steve and Robbie. Janet, however, would keep her own feelings silent and try to act compliantly, whilst her brothers enjoyed the elevated status they had been given through their suffering. One afternoon, while her other siblings were at their sports practice, Janet was at home alone with her fourteen year old brother Steve. Janet's Mum was out getting groceries; she would be coming home in an hour. Janet walked into her brother's room to deliver his clean washed and folded laundry, only to stumble upon him eating a huge stash of lollies. *"Don't you tell Mum about this, Janet!"* Steve threatened. Janet realised that the lollies must have been stolen and they both knew he was going to be in trouble if their mother found out. Without adults around, Steve erupted into a fit of anger. *"Why can't you leave me alone! You're always sticking your head in where you are not wanted! When I catch you, you're going to be in trouble!"* Janet didn't have time to be in shock, as Steve was yelling and his anger rising - and the situation - was rapidly escalating. He was chasing her around the house and when he caught Janet, he pinned her down. *"You'll be sorry for sticking your nose in where you don't belong, Janet!"* and he pushed his forearm down over her neck. Steve was out of control - he had never taken anything this far before and Janet was starting to struggle to breathe. She was banging her feet down on the floor as loudly as she could, because she couldn't scream. A knock at the door disrupted the scene and as Steve pulled back, Janet pushed herself quickly out from underneath him. Two Police Officers were standing at the door, as the neighbours had

called through fifteen minutes earlier when the running and scream-
ing had started getting loud. Janet could see the police had already
arrived, but the intensity of the scene had made the whole world spin
and she was so scared that she couldn't speak. While her brother was
being questioned by the police (who were trying to understand what
had happened), Janet was left alone in the lounge room, sitting perfectly still in shock. Janet relayed this experience to me in a mentoring
appointment and shared her devastation that even the police could not
see the truth of what had happened, and she was neither protected nor
given any comfort or reassurance.

Later on, when their mother returned home, it was Janet that was
told off for going into her brother's room unannounced. Steve had
already gotten rid of all of the stolen lollies and Janet would not have
been believed if she had spoken up. I was able to listen intently and
really observe how ill-regarded, insignificant and uncared for Janet
had felt throughout her past circumstances. There was a consistent
theme running though her life that those in a position of authority
had never looked out for her as she would have hoped and could have
expected. The police, her Mum, and other relatives had all once been
people whom Janet had looked up to and believed she could rely on.
But Janet's whole life was only tarnished with disappointment from
authority figures who consistently let her down. Ultimately Janet
realised she couldn't completely trust anyone outside of herself, and
the lack of reliability and support actually necessitated a deep reliance
on her own intuitive guidance.

Until this point of realisation, Janet had been wavering with doubt
around her own intuitive Empath ability to read situations. Her life
seemed to waver between a reluctant admission that no one could ever
be truly relied upon and an unwillingness to ever truly trust herself.
Sharing all of these precious details with me illuminated how essential
it was for Janet to finally authorise herself and be the one person she
could learn to trust to navigate her life.

Now a grown mother of three, Janet had moved far away from her own family and rarely saw them. We had been working together for a few months, really narrowing in on supporting Janet to start trusting herself more fully. Abruptly, the same pattern popped up again. Janet was teaching a Parenting Course at a local community centre. Her background had really illustrated to her the challenges that can present when feelings are not acknowledged and individual family members feel left out and rejected. She wanted to help families to respect and understand one another's needs, so that they could work together as a team to help everyone to feel safe and important. But another volunteer teacher at the centre who had joined Janet's class, stood up and spoke out loudly half way through her presentation, *"You are sharing too much of your own personal experience! This isn't professional and it's not acceptable for you to be sharing such personal information here!"* Janet stood still, shell-shocked in front of her class, feeling deeply embarrassed. The small group of parents in the class all became silent, uncomfortable and unsure of what to think. Janet tried to speak up and reply, but it just felt as though her thoughts couldn't come out clearly and her voice seemed to freeze. Having another volunteer teacher tell her that she was doing the wrong thing by sharing parts of her personal experience deeply affected Janet's confidence. After ten minutes of strange ambiguity, Janet dismissed the class and thanked everyone for coming. She got straight into her car and rushed home, feeling absolutely distraught. Janet cried profusely for hours, allowing her whole heart to break, because she was being told that she was 'wrong' yet again. She was being attacked and put down by someone who should have been there to support her.

Janet began to acknowledge that her fear of her Empathic abilities had left her speechless and feeling guilty for so long and the pain had surmounted to such an intense level, that Janet knew it was time to acknowledge the validity of her own perception. Having this gift had felt incredibly isolating, but whenever Janet was in nature she could hear the stars speak to her, she could look out at night and commune with the moon or even go on a walk and hang out with a rainbow. It was whilst in nature that Janet was able to access a sense of knowing that everything was going to be OK. There was always a sense of light that was leading Janet forward, even though she knew that there were no adults whom she could depend upon. Janet knew that the earth supported her: all of nature was looking out for her and this spoke to her in a way that Janet knew she was never actually alone.

The pain of having someone else try to make Janet 'wrong' was actually a tipping point for her to acknowledge how 'right' she was. Some adults found Janet's perceptive insight incriminating and exposing, whilst others found it insightful and illuminating. It suddenly became obvious how many people actually respected and revered Janet for her wise and insightful view. Friends and extended family members often sought out her perspective because of the accuracy her Empathic insight provided in complex personal situations. There were actually so many people around Janet who respected and admired Janet for her wisdom; it was time to 'own' the knowing that she did have the ability to perceive information that existed beyond the rational mind. By investing attention into the knowing deep inside of her belly, Janet was able to realise that part of the terror of being so deeply let down by authority figures came from the truth that she had premonitions of these situations unfolding which she chose to ignore. Janet could see that it was time to disregard the idea that she could safely assume that any authority figures had her best interests at heart; she could access all of the information and support she needed by acknowledging what she could perceive in her belly. This shift brought peace, acceptance and a huge amount of lightness and relief for Janet, as she was finally able to dismiss any idea in her mind that someone outside of her could ever possibly know more about her situation that she did.

As Empaths, we need to accept that we are our own most effective "authority figures". No one can protect, advise or govern us better than our own innate guiding instincts. When we self-authorise, we are finally able to own our knowing, to heal ourselves and to grow in strength, without external control or validation.

## *Healing Guidance:*

1. What one problem have you tried to find an **authority** to help you solve?

2. What problem in your life has been solved by **finding an answer within**?

3. Where in your life do you most need to **trust** yourself right now?

# *Healing Affirmations:*

- *I forgive those who led me astray, as I see now that they were lost*
- *My insight and awareness is always the best source of guidance*
- *Being let down by others helps me to trust myself more fully*
- *I pay attention to my inner wisdom here and now*
- *I'm grateful to come home to trusting myself*

# Chapter 11

## Shame or Mercy?

*I define 'shame' as the sense that we are 'wrong' through the lens of somebody else's perception. This reservoir of internal shame and 'wrongness' breeds a pattern of emotional secrecy, unhealthy independence and stoic self-deception, in which we mask our true authentic feelings and prefer to conjure up and pretend to be in another emotional state that may be more pleasing to our companions.*

*a*s Empaths, we are acutely aware of how others perceive us and our situation. This tendency to view ourselves through the lens of other people's emotional experiences of us contaminates our ability to see ourselves for who we truly are. As we feel the emotions others experience when we talk, share and express ourselves, it's common for Empaths to develop a sense of shame around having needs, feeling so called 'negative' emotions, as well as worrying that they are a burden and a discomfort for others. I define 'shame' as the sense that we are 'wrong' through the lens of somebody else's perception. This reservoir of internal shame and 'wrongness' breeds a pattern of emotional secrecy, unhealthy independence and stoic self-deception, in which we mask our true authentic feelings and prefer to conjure up and pretend to be in another emotional state that may be more pleasing to our companions. When we can understand that our perception of ourselves is invariably influenced by the view that others have of us, we can cleanse ourselves of the shame that so easily becomes our experience.

Isabelle had always felt deeply. She had a lifetime of experiences which were all infused with the emotional perspective of others. Her ability to perceive needs, to nurture loved ones and to shift the tide of climatic emotional scenes were all welcomed and valued aspects of this giving heart. It was Isabelle's inability to distinguish her emotions from those of people around her which proved overwhelming. Becoming dissociated from her own genuine feelings left Isabelle in a position where her daily experience of life was not her own, but was instead influenced too heavily by the emotional climates of everyone around her. This is not something that an Empath is always aware of: for awareness to be present, we need to be conscious and accepting that this is our reality. And without comparison, it's difficult to perceive this different 'take' on reality. All Empaths are born with this gift and know no other way of perceiving life, love and themselves, except through the emotional experiences of others.

Isabelle responded to her position in life by becoming diligent at lightening the mood - humour was her ally to break through the heavy stagnant emotions of others. Her kindness and genuine generosity were able to demonstrate love and to cut though challenging moments. This loving nature was how Isabelle became known throughout her community, but beneath her disposition of kindness and caring was a cavity holding unmet needs. Being so adept at providing for the needs of others meant that Isabelle herself was often overlooked. Her needs didn't seem pressing or urgent, so they were rarely considered. Now, because this had always been a normal experience for Isabelle, she came to find her place in serving others and pushing down her awareness of her own needs. Isabelle was so acutely aware of what was needed by all of those around her, was she really going to add her own needs to the mammoth pile? And even if she did, who was going to perceive those needs or could possibly respond to or provide for them? Her position of giving became the natural standpoint and coping strategy for Isabelle. While she didn't feel as though she had chosen this position, nobody else seemed to notice her predicament and it had been this way her whole life, so why dream of or yearn for anything more?

Isabelle was accustomed to her life of service; her father was from Ireland and her mother was from Australia and when her parents separated, Isabelle felt so deeply for her father that she went to live with him in Ireland when she was just 7 years old. She knew what he needed and felt that nothing was more significant than staying with him. Her father's mental health problems were obvious to everyone around him, but they didn't know what to do and so did nothing. Isabelle was devoted to her father and despite being young, knew that he needed love, care and nurture. Practical service - helping around the house, taking care of herself and being as good natured and patient as possible – were Isabelle's ways in which she could demonstrate her deep love for her father.

Living alone with an alcoholic with mental health issues exposed Isabelle to a view of life that few even know exist at such a tender age. While she was able to see past the aggression, slovenliness and poor manners, her concern for her father elevated a little more with each passing day. Weeks and months would pass by monotonously, as the two of them found a rhythm which allowed them to subsist together, despite her father's ongoing and escalating problems. By the time Isabelle was twelve, though, it was clear that this environment was deteriorating and was highly unsuitable, meaning that Isabelle would need to leave and return to live with her mother in Australia. The burden of feeling ashamed for walking away from, caring for and living with her Dad, meant that even with vast geographical space, Isabelle's guilt and worry never abated.

As an adult, Isabelle pursued a career in caring; it had always been in her nature, so getting paid to do this was a logical decision. The more experience she gained, the more she was able to understand that she had a unique ability to perceive and accommodate the emotional needs of others. Witnessing hardship, suffering and difficulty was easy for Isabelle, due to her personal background; in the medical system there was no end to the exposure of hardship that she would encounter - it mounted higher on a daily basis.

She had already met a wonderful man and had her first son now. One day, while Isabelle was transporting her son to his weekly swimming class, she became aware of sirens and saw an ambulance speeding past. The day proceeded as usual but upon returning home, Isabelle saw an ambulance sitting still in the driveway. Panic rushed through her although she knew she must slow down and pay attention.

Walking slowly and nervously forward, she met a policeman who confirmed her worst fear - her husband had been killed in an accident. Isabelle dropped to the ground wailing, totally losing control of her legs and frame as she fell limp. At the funeral, Isabelle's tears would not cease to flow and each morning there were only a few short moments before she remembered the new state of her reality, then the tears would begin again. Suddenly the circumstances of Isabelle's life had come to such a dramatic crescendo that it was no longer possible for her to be as invested in caring for others, now that her grief required more of her own attention.

The position of 'carer' had become a role that was now stifling Isabelle with mounting shame and guilt. Not only was she unable to invest as much in caring for others, but now the gaping needs calling to her from within were beginning to grow unbearably loud. First life became shallow, then it became empty and Isabelle reeled back from investing in anything. Gradually, a heavy sense of shame developed around Isabelle's own secret grief; the terrible tragedy of losing both her father and her partner could no longer be denied. It's easy for an Empath to keep their own tragedy and emotional complexity hidden from the public world, as they fear themselves to be 'too much' for anyone else to cope with. The two combatant desires to express her heart and to protect others from her emotions collided within Isabelle; the rough combination of opposing polarities became enemies which rubbed against one another perpetually. This friction was effectively eroding the internal stability and safety of Isabelle's emotional terrain.

I was fortunate to meet Isabelle at a workshop, and had the privilege of talking with her and knowing I needed to lovingly support her to become more honest with me about her true feelings. Her hot flushed cheeks were a palpable expression of her internal resistance; the desire to erupt and share was battling with the fear of exposing someone else to what she was not able to cope with herself. With Isabelle's permission, I was able to express what she was feeling and give words to the big but unspoken emotions which were filling her up within. She was shocked and looked at me with relief and fear combined. I could tell that Isabelle was checking to see if I was OK, and as she felt how grounded and calm I was staying with her in these emotions, Isabelle had a whole new experience. The shame she had always felt around the terror and distress of her loss was now shared. It was now being acknowledged, it was real and it was not necessary to keep it suppressed any more.

Over time, Isabelle was able to confide more with me and to finally find a safe space to share her feelings, experiences and perspective, knowing that she could not 'contaminate' me. As this unfolded, the associated shame around not wanting to hurt anyone with her own experience was able to abate and Isabelle was finally able to receive the support she needed to grieve her loss and to honour the memories of her dear husband and father. The spaciousness which opened up inside Isabelle was so new to her; those two competing desires to both share and conceal her pain had been reconciled and Isabelle finally achieved a sense of her worthiness to receive nurturing herself. Life opened up to a gentle state of ease as the burden of hiding her own feelings from herself was gone. There was a sense of lightness within Isabelle now, a deep assurance that nothing she felt could ever overwhelm her if it could be safely shared with someone whom she could trust.

Empaths need to find a way to confront the shame they feel and to be merciful to ourselves. Our responsibility is to develop sufficient self-worth to know that we can cope not only with our own experiences, but with those of other whom we can assist with our healing presence, through a combination of acceptance, mercy and love. We must be able to share without self-judgement, in order to convey our compassion and allow others to share and to heal through us.

## *Healing Guidance:*

1. Name a **choice** you made or a part of yourself which you were taught to **condemn or shame**.

2. Write a letter expressing a **genuine apology** for looking down on this part or choice.

3. Ask yourself which colour you can use to bring any shamed parts into **loving acceptance**.

# *Healing Affirmations:*

- *I acknowledge my shame and set myself free*
- *I deeply forgive the mistake of seeing myself as wrong*
- *I free myself from any and all lingering shame*
- *I deeply and completely hold myself in full mercy and compassion*
- *My heart swells in mercy for myself and all mankind*

# Chapter 12

## Empath Children or Born Healers?

*I allowed her to see me cry and we bonded together even more deeply, because I knew that my daughter 'knew' what I had gone through. Not just because of the verbal details that we had relayed, but because of the willingness she demonstrated to feel what I had felt.*

*I* believe we are simply born with our Empath abilities; they are with us in the womb. Investing so much time and care into owning and embracing my Empath abilities ultimately gave birth to my career. Having now invested 10 years into serving and supporting other Empaths to find their way back to their true nature as a means of untangling themselves from a myriad of difficult situations, I was now a mother and my second child was also an Empath.

I was inspired to have a second child; it felt as though a revelation came, confirming that there was somebody else watching over us who was waiting to come down and join our family and share the fun! I agreed to have this second child, but only upon the condition that I could find a way to enjoy a more relaxed, calmer birth experience. The twenty hours of labour I'd endured with my son started at a birthing centre and ended at the hospital with a half block epidural. The difficulty and immense discomfort of this experience reflected my fear of further pain and my inability to emotionally self-soothe at the time.

I was led to resources and ideas which allowed me to finally trust myself, my body and my baby to all work together to allow an effortless and beautiful birthing experience to unfold. I imagined going into labour in the morning straight after my son was safely at day care, and being able to calmly deliver a happy healthy baby by lunchtime. And just as I saw it in my mind, that was exactly what unfolded. While my husband drove our son to kindergarten at 9.00am, I knew the sensations I could feel were the indicators that I was in labour - it was time. We went straight to the birthing centre and I put on relaxing music and told everyone not to mention the time: I knew how excruciating it had been to feel pressure around 'how long' this was going to take and I knew that I needed to eradicate that concern for myself. I kept myself patiently devoted to my breath in each and every moment; the calming meditation music that played in the background was on repeat. I felt safe and supported and having no awareness of the passage of time, I was free to honour my experience, whatever it was going to be. I allowed no-one else in the room except my midwife (the same one who had helped me to deliver my first child) and my husband. Both of them were calming, soothing, very caring individuals whom I trusted and knew would support me to stay relaxed, so I could simply allow a beautiful birthing experience to unfold.

I knew it was wise to allow the sensations to move through my body; I respected that this was conducive to opening up the passageway so that my daughter could move through easily. I spoke to my daughter in my mind, just as I had throughout my whole pregnancy, knowing she could hear me. I was saying, *"It's time, let's do this together - go with the feelings you can feel - I am here, I will hold you in my arms soon. Mummy loves you so much"*. The sensations never felt like pain this time - it just felt like I was concentrating on witnessing them and trusting what they were supporting me to do. As my daughter's shoulders moved into position along my hips, I was enveloped by the most blissful all-encompassing feeling of euphoria. I surrendered and allowed the feeling to pass through my whole body, a sense of light illuminated my mind and helped me to soften for this pivotal transition. It wasn't long before my little girl was in my arms and I was in raptures, appreciating the ease of trust and the capacity we had to work together through our unique connection, to create a beautiful birth experience.

I was enchanted by my daughter from the first moment that I met her. I had felt equally as smitten with my son - it was love at first sight with both of them! But this time, for me as a woman, giving birth to my daughter gave me the genuine impression that she was akin to royalty, my own little Princess whom I would serve, honour and respect for all of my days. Bow is a highly sensitive Empath and feels everything very deeply. I learned early on to be kind, merciful and gentle with her. Any expectations, rules or cajoling would be met head-on with disapproval, defiance or crying. Learning how to honour Bow, co-create with her and understand her motivations and impulses allowed me to align myself with her goals so that we could evolve as a family.

My deepest desire was to help Bow to feel safe experiencing her own feelings within her inner emotional world; to support her to recognise and interpret her feelings so that she could rely on them from the beginning and use her gift as an Empath to support her in life. Bow is naturally very discerning, and very self-trusting. She can gauge whether someone is worthy of her trust or not very quickly. There are absolutely times when her feelings become so big that she needs support and nurture to help them to soften and release. Fortunately, I was able to invest a level of care and support in her emotionally that I have never known – a way of honouring her that has taken me years to find in my own relationship with myself.

By the age of 5, Bow was articulate, self-determined and in rapport with herself. She could take risks, express her true feelings and show me the signs she knew I could interpret, to request what she needed. As an 'Intuitive Mother', I had to break down a lot of the self-imposed ideas about 'mothering' that I formulated from my own experience of being a child. Initially my attempt at being a 'mother' correlated with a very 'repeat the past or over-compensate with the exact opposite' model of parenting which I had to swiftly disarm and release. Some of my own painful memories would cause me to swing resolutely into a position of *"I will not repeat that"*, only to violently swing back toward the other direction when my self-pity asserted *"But this is all that I have ever known!"*. I truly required generous lashings of compassion whilst I found my true centre as a parent! Ultimately, my model for parenting came from the simple idea that 'being who I am' is the most powerful way I can best serve and care for my children. I believe that's what my children need most - a mother who is in her truth. Coming to this realisation was a vulnerable and scary transition at times, because I wasn't always sure how my children would respond to the openly vulnerable and truly imperfect individual that I am. However, my honesty and vulnerability have been rewarded with a kind and soft rapport in which my children feel safe to be even more of who they really are and are able to hold me in mercy as I allow myself to simply be who I am as their mother. As I hold my children in compassion, they too respond by holding me in compassion and step by step, inch by inch, we have all revealed far more to one other than I ever knew was possible in a family.

My daughter has a great love for drawing; it's often a way that she goes within herself. I love to see how she enjoys expressing herself through patterns, colours and drawings. One occasion in particular allowed me to see the real blessing of having a family life established on foundations of authenticity, asking and receiving, clear boundaries and a willingness to honour one another's true nature. Bow brought out a picture that she said she had drawn for me. It was a picture of a woman crying with a small baby inside of her. Just a simple stick figure pencil illustration, it had a huge effect on me as I knew what my daughter was conveying. She was witnessing me with compassion. We didn't share with many friends or extended family members that our first child was miscarried, but it was something that we openly told our children, because we decided that we wanted to trust our children with the truth. Bow knew that she had an older brother who had been miscarried. But the drawing conveyed a depth of emotional perception that moved me very deeply. The picture of me crying while still having the baby inside perfectly reflected my experience, because even before the cramps came to eject our baby from my body, I knew that he had died (I also knew he was a boy, our first son). I had cried before our baby left my body and now my daughter was witnessing back for me. No one had been mentioned this experience for months before Bow drew it this one day. I was struck by the gentle compassionate love that my child now invested in me as she showed me that she knew what I had experienced. Bow was sad, but she didn't cry; I bent down onto my knees and thanked her and held her close. I allowed her to see me cry and we bonded together even more deeply, because I knew that my daughter 'knew' what I had gone through. Not just because of the verbal details that we had relayed, but because of the willingness she demonstrated to feel what I had felt. What struck me about this experience was how genuine and sincere Bow's act of love was; seeing how my daughter had decided to stay with me and allow herself to stay in the feeling of loss and grief with me illustrated her depth of love. I had always tried to stay with my daughter in her emotional experiences and to reassure or comfort her, but even now, as a small 5 year old, she was able to offer this to me voluntarily and the shift that I felt was unmistakeable. My child was willing to feel what I had felt in order to show me her love. This is the gift of an Empath child; they are born healers in the womb, capable of bravely and wisely staying with us in our truth as we bravely stay with them in their truth.

I feel incredibly fortunate to have this experience and be able to relay to you the profound impact that these principles can have in our lives. It is my hope that we can honour our own Empath nature and slowly but surely trust in our truth, to cultivate a reverence and respect for the abilities that being an Empath gives us. As we focus on accepting the depth and breadth of what it means to be an Empath, I believe our genuine living example is the best way to offer new, insightful opportunities to our children and to everyone else around us. Allowing our children to see vulnerable, authentic examples of how we can share our true feelings within the family home will transform the future for them. It's my most sincere wish that we can support Empath children to feel safe, supported and cared for and to experience all of their feelings. Then we may be able to show them how to use the precious information these feelings carry to become more discerning, aware and connected to their individual truth; that they can cherish and honour their Empath nature and be able to impart their healing presence out into the world is my deepest desire.

# *Healing Guidance:*

1. Have you ever felt **seen and witnessed** by a child?

2. What traits can you remember in yourself as a child, that can help you to **see and own** that you are an Empath now?

3. What needs to start **changing** in your life, so that you can start **honouring yourself** as a natural healer?

Lysa Black

# *Healing Affirmations:*

- *I have always seen the truth in others*
- *My inner child offers me healing presence*
- *I feel and trust in my knowing*
- *Children are born wise and clear*
- *Innocence and purity hold the truth for us all*

123

# Chapter 13

## Empath Purpose: Healing Presence

*Nothing less than the genuine experience of truly being seen, accepted, loved and embraced in our vulnerable truth is capable of translating compassionate presence to our hearts. We cannot give that which we have not yet received.*

$\mathscr{T}$he truth ultimately reveals itself that, as Empaths, we were not abandoned and cast aside to endure so much tragedy without the grace of a divine purpose. Instead, we were led along a course that would eventually reveal to us the true value of our gift. The tragedy that befalls us ultimately cultivates our healing presence and once we recognise how devoid and barren some moments, people and cultures are of compassion, we are able to develop the capacity to meet the requirements of our own soul. Ultimately our liberation comes from becoming what we individually needed the most.

Teejay was a gentle hearted man who was seeking mentoring to help him to embody his purpose and heal from his past. He was able to feel the emotions of others and this had always been a deeply confusing and disorientating experience for him. With confirmation and guidance, Teejay was supported to honour his true nature as an Empath. The realities of energy and emotion was not acknowledged in his childhood home and the weighty expectations around who he needed to become were a constant source of excruciating judgment and overwhelming pressure. The patriarchal line of his culture assumed that men were supposed to be tough, unfeeling and decidedly hard. To be a 'real' man, one must 'push' and 'assert' his own agenda. Teejay failed to live up to the expectations that were placed on him; lack of appreciation for his gentle, deeply feeling and intuitive disposition left him feeling weak, vulnerable and exposed.

Now, as a grown adult, Teejay was able to craft a life that would nourish and support him in his truth. He always knew it was impossible to live up to the expectations that others placed on him; being supported to honour his true nature opened Teejay up to a playful and supportive new rhythm to live his life by. Accepting that crowds and groups of strangers were not supportive for Teejay's sensitive nature allowed him to begin erecting some clear boundaries around himself, so that he could trust that there was a way to feel strong and secure as he found a home within himself. He learnt to truly trust that if it didn't feel right, he simply wouldn't go to a place, share food or spend time with some people. Honouring these choices gave Teejay a sense of clarity and safety, so that he could speak up, express his boundaries and support himself.

The trauma that remained from being repeatedly yelled at, ridiculed and undermined whilst growing up meant that seemingly innocent unfoldings in Teejay's adult life would result in emotional overwhelm. Teejay would lose sight of his own perception and become engulfed in an ego-led barrage of intimidation and cruelty which left him weak and depleted. Whether this lasted for hours, days or weeks, Teejay was incapable of feeling steady on his feet under certain circumstances. Together, we were able to cultivate the trust and honesty to speak truthfully about what was happening when Teejay felt triggered. As I demonstrated my willingness to hold Teejay in mercy and compassion, he was able to connect with his true essence and articulate the truth that he could perceive from within himself. The more comfortable Teejay became admitting the truth to me, the more he realised admitting it to himself and speaking the truth from his own perspective were the keys to freeing himself from the web of cruelty and undermining deception that his ego would attempt to cloak the situation with.

On one occasion, Teejay was locked in a memory of himself as a 3 year old child. While learning to ride his trike, Teejay got close to a slope in the driveway and as he haphazardly slid, he accidentally bumped into his father's car. Even at his young age, Teejay knew this vehicle was his father's pride and joy and that he was therefore in big trouble. In this situation, Teejay experienced the full force of his father's explosive rage. I could perceive Teejay as a little 3 year old boy frozen by fear, and I spoke calmly and softly, staying close and reassuring Teejay that I was right by his side. As horrible as it was to reflect on this memory, I was willing to stay with him and experience the depth of Teejay's emotion with him. He was apprehensive and nervous that I would criticise him and tell him to do something to change the scene in his mind. Physically frozen by fear, he was silent and unable to express his perspective or be very conscious of what was happening within him. This paralyzing terror kept him still and this stillness was all that Teejay could be aware of.

I could feel myself joining Teejay in this scene. It was like watching a dream and while I knew I wasn't really there, I was able to connect with this little child and offer compassionate presence. As this small boy sat silent and still, I slowed down my breathing and became more present and still inside. I allowed myself to feel the depth of what Teejay was experiencing in this moment, but I didn't wince. I allowed the sensations to be present with me as I beamed love in on Teejay. Slowly but surely he was able to sink into his body and was able to feel safe, knowing how appropriate and understandable it was for him to feel afraid. Knowing that someone else was with him, who was actively choosing to stay and offer him love, created a huge shift for Teejay, toward a genuine sense of feeling loved, cared for and supported. After decades of being treated terribly, just one moment of truly receiving compassionate presence was able to help Teejay return to his body and experience something profound.

Nothing less than the genuine experience of truly being seen, accepted, loved and embraced in our vulnerable truth is capable of translating compassionate presence to our hearts. We cannot give that which we have not yet received. And from the moment that Teejay truly received compassionate presence, he could offer it to himself and others. I was fortunate to later hear of examples in which Teejay could extend compassionate presence to stray animals and witness how their behaviour changed when he did. From animals to strangers on the street, to personal friends and professional clients, Teejay was now in a position in which he could sense the judgement rising up within. Through observation, Teejay developed his ability to surrender judgement, embrace the truth of 'what was' and soften into compassion, allowing 'what was' to simply 'be'. Repeatedly, Teejay was able to navigate his way out of unconscious judgment and back into compassionate presence.

Six months later, I was in the unfortunate position of losing our pet foal. Our mare, whom we had hand-reared as a new-born was now 3 years old and was expecting her very own foal. This pregnancy was a huge blessing for my whole family, and we had been anticipating the arrival of this little foal with great rapture and wonder. Sadly, the foal was born but died the very next day. I was heart-broken and shattered to see this much anticipated joyful arrival become a devastating loss; the grief struck me harder than I knew how to bear. I felt prompted to reach out to Teejay and share the news of what had happened. Initially it was difficult for Teejay to be fully present to this information. But within 24 hours, I received a message of deep compassion back in reply. I was now being witnessed and held in compassionate presence by my client.

Teejay relayed the truth about how difficult it was for him to accept and acknowledge this sad turn of events. The depth of emotion around it was initially uncomfortable and he had to choose to allow himself to actually feel it. Once Teejay did permit himself to sink into the feelings about the loss of this foal, he could expand into the spaciousness of compassion which allowed his heart to swell and send me comfort and care. What a beautiful full circle experience of the power of investing compassionate presence in others; I never anticipated that what I had given to Teejay would now be returning to me amplified. Feeling his genuine care and compassionate presence, I was comforted and supported through the depths of my sadness, knowing that I was not alone. Personally, I am more comfortable being in the giving position and so receiving this love was incredibly humbling and soul stirring for me. It truly helped me to capture the significance of being able to offer compassionate healing presence, because what we give to another will ultimately return back in return.

Teejay's ability to offer himself compassionate presence also deepened. When he was scared, triggered or afraid, he was able to reach in, stay within himself, perceive what had happened and then remind himself of the truth, which ultimately cultivated an enhanced level of awareness and insight. By accommodating and supporting his true nature, Teejay was able to transform all of the past hurt into a deep acceptance of his true nature and a willingness to now support himself. Teejay now has a masterful capacity to stay with himself, to observe without judgment and adopt playful curiosity that allows him to not only offer himself healing presence, but likewise offer it to everyone near him, including me.

The timeless adage "Healer, heal thyself" is particularly true for Empaths, because it is only through cultivating self-compassion, self-authorisation and inward mercy that we are able to effectively address the feelings and experiences of others and to offer remedies which will share our healing presence with the world.

# *Healing Guidance:*

1. What does healing presence **mean** to you?

2. How has your **past pain** prepared you to **cultivate** your own healing presence?

3. What do you have **permission** to do or to **change** in your life now that you know you are an Empath?

# *Healing Affirmations:*

- *Loving compassion surrounds me and all that I do*
- *I breathe in and offer healing presence to all*
- *It's in my nature to bring healing presence*
- *I own and embrace my natural healing gift*
- *I emanate healing presence*

# Closing Story

# Quan Yin, The Goddess of Compassion

uan Yin is renowned throughout Asia as the Goddess of Compassion. Revered as the feminine counterpart of Buddha, her story shows us the fullest expression of what is possible as we cultivate our empath nature and rise on purpose.

After realising that she was powerless to create change in anyone outside herself, Quan Yin devoted her life to self-mastery. She invested her awareness, her love and compassion within to transform her own experience. Quan Yin was so dedicated to holding herself in an abundance of love that she emanated healing presence wherever she went.

At the completion of her mortal sojourn, Quan Yin was rising to walk the staircase to heaven when she turned back to see mankind suffering and writhing in distress. She chose to delay her ascension and return, to simply sit and be with humanity. Allowing herself to be an presence of embodied grace, compassion and mercy, she was a shining soul of light.

Quan Yin's example is an inspiration to ignite the potential within us. Her emanation of love and compassion is a demonstration of the inherent capacity for all of humanity to embody their truth so fully that it serves to liberate others. To hold so much compassion that, simply by being near you, others may spontaneously experience the transformational healing power you hold within you, as an Empath Healer.

# *Healing Affirmations:*

- *I was born to bring truth to light*
- *It's in my nature to bring healing presence*
- *My being alone supports others to self-heal*
- *My being creates space in which spontaneous healing happens effortlessly*
- *I witness and acknowledge the healing effects of my presence*

Made in the USA
Columbia, SC
20 April 2022